LEONARDO DA VINCI
and the Renaissance in World History

Allison Lassieur

Enslow Publishers, Inc.

40 Industrial Road   PO Box 38
Box 398   Aldershot
Berkeley Heights, NJ 07922   Hants GU12 6BP
USA   UK

http://www.enslow.com

Library of Congress Cataloging-in-Publication Data

Lassieur, Allison.
  Leonardo da Vinci and the Renaissance in world history / Allison
Lassieur.
    p. cm. — (In world history)
    Includes bibliographical references (p.) and index.
    Summary: Traces the life and times of Leonardo da Vinci showing his
effect on the world of art and on the history of the Italian Renaissance.
    ISBN 0-7660-1401-0
    1. Leonardo, da Vinci, 1452–1519—Juvenile literature.
  2. Renaissance—Italy—Juvenile literature. 3. Artists—Italy—Biography—
Juvenile literature. [1. Leonardo, da Vinci, 1452–1519. 2. Renaissance—
Italy. 3. Artists.] I. Title. II. Series.
N6923.L33 L38 2000
709'.2—dc21

                                              99-050571

Printed in the United States of America

10 9 8 7 6 5 4 3 2 1

To Our Readers:
All Internet addresses in this book were active and appropriate when we
went to press. Any comments or suggestions can be sent by e-mail to
Comments@enslow.com or to the address on the back cover.

Illustration Credits: Braun and Schneider, *Historic Costume in Pictures*
(New York: Dover Publications, Inc., 1975), p. 24; Charles D. O'Malley
and J. B. de C. M. Saunders, *Leonardo on the Human Body* (New York:
Dover Publications, Inc., 1983), pp. 75, 77; Corel Corporation, pp. 6, 37,
40, 43, 48, 51, 55, 59, 89, 99; Enslow Publishers, Inc., p. 35; Gustave
Doré, *Doré's Illustrations of the Crusades* (Mineola, N.Y.: Dover
Publications, Inc., 1997), p. 10; Jean Paul Richter, *The Notebooks of
Leonardo da Vinci*, 2 vols. (New York: Dover Publications, Inc., 1970),
pp. 53, 63, 82, 86, 88, 107, 113; J. G. Heck, *The Complete Encyclopedia of
Illustration* (New York: Park Lane, 1979), p. 8; Library of Congress,
p. 117.

Cover Illustration: Jean Paul Richter, *The Notebooks of Leonardo da
Vinci* (New York: Dover Publications, Inc., 1970), vol. 1 (Portrait—
Leonardo da Vinci); Digital Vision Ltd. (Background—Map).

Every effort has been made to locate the copyright owners of all the
pictures used in this book. If due acknowledgment has not been made,
we sincerely regret the omission.

Contents

Chapter 1

Buried Treasure in Their Own House

Magnificent art. Amazing inventions. Scientific marvels. The Renaissance in Italy—which lasted roughly from 1300 to 1550—was an exciting time to be alive. The people who lived then knew how extraordinary it was. Fifteenth-century humanist Matteo Palmieri wrote that he had been "born in this new age, so full of hope and promise, which already rejoices in a greater array of nobly-gifted souls than the world has seen in the thousand years that have preceded it."[1]

Into this exciting time came Leonardo da Vinci. When he was born in the mid-1400s, Italy was riding a great wave of culture, power, and thought. Cities were spending vast sums on public artworks. Religious orders hired artisans to decorate their cathedrals and monasteries. Artistic ideas flowed through every part of this new world.

By the time of the Renaissance, Rome was already a city filled with the crumbling art and buildings of years past, such as the Coliseum.

Renaissance is a French word meaning rebirth. The first person to use the term was historian Giorgio Vasari, who, in 1550, used the word *rinascita* (rebirth) to describe the time in which he lived. To people of the Renaissance, this term meant a rebirth of the ideas and art of ancient Greece and Rome that had been forgotten during the Middle Ages.

Renaissance scholars called the time before the Renaissance the Dark Ages. They believed that the light of knowledge had disappeared. We know today that the knowledge of ancient cultures never

6

disappeared completely. After the fall of Rome in A.D. 476, the Germanic tribes that conquered Rome adopted much of Roman culture. However, much of Roman and Greek science, technology, and learning was forgotten. Some of the learning was kept alive by medieval monks, who painstakingly copied ancient texts. Gradually, scholars forgot how to read classical Latin and Greek. Texts were lost, destroyed, or ignored.

Although medieval scholars had begun to rediscover some of the glory of ancient Rome as early as the twelfth century, things really began to change in the 1300s. The first rumblings of change began in Rome. Romans had always been surrounded by the past. Their city was full of crumbling buildings and ancient monuments. These stone ghosts hinted at the magnificence of the past. Ancient manuscripts still existed in the libraries. When scholars found these manuscripts, they were astonished. Historian John R. Hale described what their excitement must have been like:

> They were searching in libraries for forgotten manuscripts and reading them with scholarly zest. . . . This . . . gave the Renaissance a firsthand knowledge of what the ancients had actually said and enabled it to speak with them, directly, across the centuries. . . . The Italian humanists were discovering their own ancestors, finding buried treasure in their own house.[2]

The Renaissance was much more than the rediscovery of the grandeur of ancient Rome. This rebirth of ideas was not enough. People such as da Vinci turned these ideas into actions. They used the knowledge of the past to create greatness in their own time.

To understand how the Renaissance developed, it is important to know what came before it. The Middle Ages was glorious in its own way. It was the age of kings and castles, of knights and warfare, of dangerous battles and courtly love. Kings fought one another for control of land. The king rewarded trusted knights by giving them land. But these new landowners were required to provide the king with food, troops, or taxes whenever they were needed. In this way, the king still

The years before the beginning of the Renaissance were known as the Middle Ages. It was the time of chivalry, knights, and kings.

controlled his kingdom. This contract between the ruler and the nobles was called feudalism.

By the end of the Middle Ages, feudalism began to crumble. Powerful dukes and barons—the people to whom the kings had given land—fought among themselves for more power. Cities such as London and Paris grew. The Roman Catholic Church felt its power weakening. And disasters such as the Black Plague, which killed one third of the population of Europe, weakened some kings' power by killing off the farmers who grew food and paid taxes. All these events opened the door to new ideas about government and politics.

Meanwhile, people by the thousands set out to the Middle East on crusade. Christians considered Jerusalem part of their Holy Land. They often went on pilgrimages to visit this heavenly place. In the eleventh century, the Muslims, who controlled Jerusalem, forbade Christians from entering the city. The Crusades, a series of European invasions that lasted from the eleventh to the fourteenth century, were launched to win back the Holy Land from the Muslims. Waves of European armies tramped through Italy on the way to Jerusalem. When they returned, they brought with them silks, spices, exotic animals, and strange new customs. The Crusades reminded the European world that the light of culture and learning was still bright in other places.

Gradually, Italian cities such as Florence, Venice, and Rome became powerful. They became merchant cities. They took advantage of new markets in Europe

The people of Europe discovered vast sources of wealth and luxurious goods when they went on the Crusades to the Middle East and the Holy Land.

that were rising to replace feudalism. Banking and manufacturing became vital as wealth poured in.

City populations exploded. Artisans, merchants, businessmen, and scholars were drawn to these cities as centers of learning and culture. For the first time in history, an individual did not have to be rich, powerful, or royal to live comfortably in a big city. People no longer had to work for kings or landed nobles. Along with this growing freedom came a new desire to express bold ideas and to create new kinds of art.

In many ways, Leonardo da Vinci is the perfect symbol of the Renaissance. He was truly unlimited by the narrow thinking of the past. He took learning to new levels never before imagined. His art showed that painting could show depth, personality, and emotion. He observed nature and developed scientific concepts that would not be rediscovered for hundreds of years. His sharp mind designed hundreds of inventions. Da Vinci rose to become the most famous artist, sculptor, engineer, and scientist of the Renaissance. In his own time, he was renowned. Today, after almost five hundred years, he is still considered one of the greatest geniuses the world has ever seen. To follow his life is to follow the path of the Renaissance, to discover this "new age, so full of hope" that changed the world then—and continues to shape it today.

Chapter 2

Life in a
New World

*A grandson of mine was born, son of Ser Piero my son, on April 15,
Saturday at three o'clock in the night. His name was Lionardo.*

—Ser Antonio da Vinci [1]

This simple sentence, jotted down in the spring of
1452, recorded the birth of a child who would someday
become one of the world's greatest men. But on that
day, Leonardo da Vinci was merely the illegitimate
son of Ser Piero da Vinci and a woman named
Caterina.

Ser Piero was a twenty-five-year-old notary in the
small Italian village of Vinci, a few miles west of
Florence. His family had been established in Vinci
as early as the thirteenth century. His ancestors were
shrewd businessmen who had become upper-middle-
class landowners. Their success had enabled them to
use the title *Ser*, which fell to Leonardo's father. [2]

Notaries could be addressed by the title *Ser*, which was similar to the title *Mr.* today.

Very little is known about Leonardo's mother, Caterina. Some histories refer to her as a peasant girl. Few other details have ever been recorded. It is clear, though, that Ser Piero did not intend to marry the mother of his son. Soon after Leonardo's birth, Piero married sixteen-year-old Albiera Amadori. Town records note that Caterina married a local potter named Accattabriga the following year. She then moved with him to a nearby town.

Scholars are not certain about the details of Leonardo da Vinci's early life. He probably lived with his mother and stepfather, as most infants and small children would have done. Da Vinci himself never wrote about what happened when he was young, and there are no other records that might reveal details about his early years. But by the time the boy was five, tax records indicate that he was living in his father's house.

Illegitimate Children

The circumstances of da Vinci's birth were not very unusual for the time. It was common during the Renaissance, as it has been throughout history, for children to be born of parents who were not married. It was not considered shameful to be illegitimate. Fathers regularly acknowledged their children by other women, and sons were especially cherished. Many times, as in da Vinci's case, fathers raised their illegitimate children in their own homes, along with their legitimate children.

Growing Up in the Renaissance

For families of the middle and upper classes, the birth of a new baby was cause for great celebration. The new mother was showered with expensive gifts and food. The baby might be wrapped in expensive cloth made of gold or embroidered with pearls and jewels, depending on the wealth of the family.

As soon as they could walk, children were dressed like adults and encouraged to learn from the adults around them. Children were encouraged to discover their own individuality. Da Vinci, like other children raised in the country, probably explored the breathtaking Italian countryside, which was filled with vineyards, clear brooks, and shady groves. He was allowed to paint and draw. Early on, Ser Piero noticed his son's great talent.

A legend from da Vinci's childhood recounts an incident in which a local peasant approached Ser Piero and asked him to paint a shield. Ser Piero agreed. He took the shield to his son, who agreed to paint something on it. The young da Vinci painted a grotesque creature. It was so lifelike that his father ran from the room in fear when he saw the finished painting. Ser Piero had Leonardo paint another shield with a simple design, which he gave to the grateful peasant. Then, he secretly sold his son's amazing work.

Toys and Games

When they were not at their lessons, children such as Leonardo played games that many children would recognize today. A wonderful painting by Renaissance artist Pieter Brueghel the Elder, called *Children's Games*, shows a crowd of Renaissance children playing leapfrog, chase, and tug-of-war. Some children swing from a post. In the background, a child climbs a tree.

Children and grown-ups also played indoor games such as chess and backgammon. People enjoyed a form of charades in which a person pulled a drawing from a bag and had to guess what it was. There was even a lively form of the "telephone" game. A group formed a circle, then one person whispered a sentence into the ear of the person beside him or her. The sentence was passed around until it came back, completely mangled, to the person who first said it.

School in the Renaissance

The Renaissance was a time when people began to believe less in the idea that one's destiny was set from birth. They came to believe more that a person could make his or her own future. People grew wealthy from business. Many had the time and money for education. Fathers were encouraged to observe their children and determine which occupations might suit them.

For most younger children, this meant school. A basic education was very important to the people of the Renaissance. Almost every town in Italy had a school. At first, many of these schools were run by the local church. But as a condition to attend these schools, families had to promise that their sons would become monks. Eventually "lay" schools, or schools open to everyone, were established. Most families paid the school to teach their children. Sometimes local guilds (organizations of craftsmen or laborers) paid for low-income children to attend.

As a child, Leonardo attended school, as did almost all children at that time. He went to a neighborhood school, where he enjoyed mathematics, music, and drawing. He delighted his father by singing and playing the lute, a guitarlike instrument.[3]

Unlike the Middle Ages, when girls were not allowed to attend school, both boys and girls attended lay schools during the Renaissance. The main purpose of school was to prepare boys for an apprenticeship, or training, to learn a profession. School gave girls the skills they would need to run a household when they were married.

Renaissance schools were very different from schools today. Instead of a large building, Renaissance schools could be just a room in a teacher's home. Students gathered each day to learn reading and arithmetic, the two basic subjects that everyone needed to know. Most students learned to read Latin, the standard language of writing and science. But students were also encouraged to learn to read and write Italian and Greek.

Sometimes wealthy Italians hired private tutors for their children. These highly respected teachers might live with their students until they grew up and either married or attended a university. Grateful parents sometimes rewarded good teachers by giving them houses and a yearly income. The best teachers might even accept students from outside the family, who would live in the teacher's house.

Students who wanted to continue their studies might go to universities. Although there had been a few places of higher learning scattered throughout Europe, it was not until the Renaissance that such institutions

Source Document

We call those studies liberal which are worthy of a free man, those studies by which we attain and practice virtue and wisdom; that education which calls forth, trains and develops those highest gifts of body and of mind which ennoble men, and which are rightly judged to rank next in dignity to virtue only. For to a vulgar temper gain and pleasure are the one aim of existence, to a lofty nature, moral worth and fame. It is, then, of the highest importance that even from infancy this aim, this effort, should constantly be kept alive in growing minds.[4]

During the Renaissance, progressive ideas about education led people to accept the idea of both boys and girls attending school. New schooling ideas also changed the type of subjects students learned, as discussed in this letter.

became widely available. These new universities, which were usually sponsored by the authorities of a particular town, were open to any citizen who could pay to attend. Some students studied full time, renting rooms while they attended classes. Laborers and merchants might also attend a class to brush up on their Latin or Greek.

Education provided opportunities for common citizens to become wealthy and important. The state demanded that its servants be educated and competent. The administrators, counselors, and advisors were often men of lowly birth who had a good education.[5]

Marriage and Family Life

Marriage and children were the goals of a great many people during the Renaissance. One member of the clergy said, "Take a wife, a beautiful wife, well-built, good-tempered, wise, and one who will give you many children. Sad is the life of a man who stays alone."[6] Marriage was so important that, in some areas, no public office could be held by a man who had not married by the time he was twenty-seven years old.

Girls were considered ready to marry when they were about twelve, but most people agreed that the best time for a girl to marry was when she was sixteen or seventeen. Parents of daughters were expected to provide a dowry, or money and goods, to the new husband. In some cases, especially in families with many daughters, paying the dowries could lead to financial ruin. Families who did not have enough money frequently forced their daughters to join a convent.

Most families, however, saw the dowry as a duty and paid it. In Florence, fathers who might not have enough money could invest in a dowry bank. When a daughter was born, a father could buy stock. After fifteen years, the stocks matured, and the father could withdraw his money to pay his daughter's dowry.

A girl could be betrothed (engaged) at the age of three, but marriage was delayed until she was twelve. In the early days of the Renaissance, a girl who was not engaged by the time she was fifteen was a disgrace. By the 1500s, the "age of disgrace" had risen to seventeen, to provide enough time for education.[7] Even with all these rules, girls were not forced to marry against their will. They had the option to reject the man their family chose.

Most people wanted to marry for love. One man tenderly wrote of his wife, "I thank Our Lord . . . for an equally excellent wife, who loved me truly, and cared most faithfully for both household and children; who was spared to me for many years, and whose death has been the greatest loss that ever has or could have befallen me."[8]

When two people decided to marry, it was customary for the man to give his lady betrothal gifts, including jewelry. One of the first documented diamond engagement rings was presented to Mary of Modina in Venice in 1503.[9] A public official, such as a notary, presided over a wedding. For lower-class families, weddings usually included a short ceremony and perhaps a wedding breakfast. But wealthy families threw great wedding celebrations with banquets, dancing, and food.

A festive wedding-day tradition was for guests and friends of the couple to carry them to their marriage bed after the wedding. One Renaissance wedding guest wrote,

> we stood talking for awhile, and then the bride and groom were put to bed, and we all went up with them right to the bed, laughing at them. It seemed strange to both of them to see so many people around their bed, all saying some pretty thing as they usually do in these cases.[10]

Renaissance Homes

After a man and woman were married, they usually settled down in a home of their own. In large cities, families lived in three- or four-story homes, similar to modern townhouses. Each level was a single room divided into smaller rooms with wooden partitions or heavy draperies. The downstairs room was usually a combination of a kitchen and dining room, with a huge fireplace. The upper floors were where the family slept. There was no living room in a Renaissance home. It was common for the lord and lady of the house to receive guests in their bedroom.

Renaissance homes were sparsely furnished by today's standards. In the kitchen, there might be a long table and chairs or benches. In their bedrooms, people kept their clothing in heavy wooden chests that might be carved or painted with scenes from the Bible or from everyday life.

The Renaissance was a time of new wealth, when almost every family could afford a few special things for the home. Tapestries from Flanders, silk from the Far East, a precious mirror made of glass, or even a small book or two, were not uncommon objects in a typical Renaissance home. Life was far from luxurious, but it could be quite comfortable.

Food and Drink

The explosion in trade brought exotic spices and new foods to Renaissance tables. Potatoes and corn arrived from the Americas. Everyone drank ale and light wine, because freshwater was hard to come by in the larger cities. In Florence, for example, each person drank about a hundred gallons of wine each year.[11] Everyone ate venison, beef, fowl, and fish. It was not uncommon to serve baked swan or pickled eels.

Poorer people had to make do with salted and pickled meats and what greens they might grow or pick in the wild. In hard times, the poor might eat turnips and bread made from grinding nuts or tree bark into flour. The lack of green vegetables was probably responsible for many of the skin diseases that fell under the heading of leprosy.[12]

Men and Women in the Renaissance

The wealth that poured into Italy during the Renaissance created a vibrant middle class of men and women. These people had enough money to pursue higher learning and enough leisure time to enjoy it. The ideal of the Renaissance was the *uomo universale*, or "universal man." According to popular thinking of the time, the universal man of society should be at home in all sports, such as running, leaping, swimming, and wrestling. He should be a good dancer and horseback rider. He should speak several languages, including Latin and Italian, and be familiar with literature and the arts.[13] Today, the term *Renaissance man* means a person who is well versed in a wide variety of subjects: art, culture, history, and politics. The term also suggests refinement and style.

For women in the Renaissance, life could be a painful contradiction. On the one hand, the exciting world of learning was open to them in ways that it had never been before. Girls went to school and studied mathematics, languages, and philosophy alongside boys. But women were not allowed to participate in many of the professions that were open to men.

Women overcame this problem in a number of ways. Some chose the religious life, rising to power as the head of a convent. Other women chose the life of a courtesan. Courtesans were wealthy prostitutes known for their beauty, refinement, and wit. Other women, especially those from important families, influenced politics and culture through their husbands, sons, and the wealth of their families.

The vast majority of women, however, worked at a trade. Many of these women toiled in small shops beside their husbands as weavers, blacksmiths, tailors, and coopers (barrel makers). As the Renaissance progressed, the small workshops were gradually replaced by large professional workshops. In the later years of the Renaissance, women were forbidden to work in public. It was considered disgraceful and a threat to a successful marriage. Women still worked, but they did so at lower-paying jobs that could be done within their homes, such as spinning thread for cloth.

Clothing of the Renaissance

During the Renaissance, Italy became the textile trading and manufacturing center of Europe. Italian wool was considered the best in the world. Silks and brocades from Florence and Milan were exported throughout the world. As one historian noted, "It is nevertheless beyond a doubt that nowhere was so much importance attached to dress as in Italy."[14]

The rise of the wealthy middle class, combined with the availability of fabrics that were once only worn by royalty, gave all Italians the chance to dress well. In both Venice and Florence, rules controlled what both men and women wore. In places where fashions were freer, such as Naples, moralists confessed with regret that no difference could be seen between nobles and middle-class citizens.[15]

Although different styles went in and out of fashion during the Renaissance, the basic wardrobe stayed the same. Men dressed in loose shirts that were bleached white. They had long, full sleeves and round

Men and women of the Renaissance generally dressed in one type of clothing, based on gender.

necklines. Over this they might wear a tight-fitting jacket called a doublet. It was made of silk, wool, or leather, and had sleeves that tied on at the shoulders. Well-dressed Italian men wore hose on their legs, which were tied to the doublet at the waist. Over this outfit a man might wear an overtunic, which was a long coatlike garment that opened in front.

A fashionable woman wore a loose-fitting white undergarment called a chemise. It had long, full sleeves and hung to the calf. Over this she wore a heavy dress with a snug-fitting bodice (top) and a skirt sewn into pleats. Over all this a woman wore a long, loose gown of velvet or brocade that hung from the shoulders in graceful drapes.

This was the world into which Leonardo da Vinci was born. He spent his childhood in a comfortable stone house in Vinci, which had belonged to his father's family for generations. Although da Vinci did not mention his childhood in any of his writings, it is likely that he enjoyed the life of a beloved son in an upper-middle-class family that could afford to dress nicely, eat good food, and live in comfort and style.

Chapter 3

City Life

Observe how much grace and sweetness are to be seen in the faces of men and women on the streets, with the approach of evening in bad weather.

—Leonardo da Vinci[1]

By the time Leonardo was a teenager, his father was keenly aware of his great talents. Historian Giorgio Vasari wrote,

> His father, Ser Piero, . . . took some of Leonardo's drawings to Andrea del Verrocchio, his intimate friend. He begged Andrea to tell him whether the boy showed promise. Verrocchio was amazed at these early efforts of Leonardo's and advised Ser Piero to see to it that his son become a painter. Leonardo was therefore sent to study in the shop of Andrea.[2]

At about age fourteen, Leonardo traveled to the bustling city of Florence to begin his artistic training as an apprentice to Andrea del Verrocchio. Verrocchio was one of the Renaissance's most famous artists. Not only was he a respected painter, but he was also a skilled goldsmith, sculptor, mathematician, and musician. His workshop, or *bottega*, was a successful example of a Florentine artist's business.

A bottega "united all the arts into one workshop." An artist might be working on the design of a church or palace in one corner of the room, while others carved or cast statues, sketched or painted pictures, cut or set gems, or carved or inlaid ivory or wood. Yet others might be fusing or beating metal, or even making a float or costumes for a festival.[3] In this atmosphere, da Vinci began his training.

Apprentices

Once a boy and his family settled on a trade, his father usually approached a master in that trade, as Ser Piero had done. If the boy showed skill and a willingness to learn, he went to live with the master. The boy worked for him in exchange for learning the trade.

Da Vinci came to Verrocchio as an apprentice. During the Renaissance, many boys were apprenticed to masters at about age fourteen, the age when da Vinci began his apprenticeship. Most artist apprentices served about six years, learning the trade and becoming skilled enough to take on commissions of their own.

An apprentice's work was long and hard, especially for the first few years of an apprenticeship. A new artist's apprentice had to sweep floors, clean brushes and other tools, mix colors, and help the more experienced apprentices with larger jobs.

In 1458, a writer named Benedetto Cotrugli published a treatise called *On Trade and the Perfect Merchant*. In it, he described a typical apprenticeship:

> Nowadays the practical Genoese and Florentines and Venetians . . . are in the habit of handing their sons over to middle-class citizens to be brought up and put in some good post, so that from childhood they may be instructed in a trade. . . . I have seen them practicing their profession not only in the menial tasks which their job involves, but even sweeping inside the shop without shame.[4]

There were many rules governing apprentices. Apprentices could not work for anyone but their masters or leave their jobs without permission. Masters agreed to give apprentices food, a place to stay, and sometimes clothing, in exchange for their work. Apprentices were expected to contribute to the different projects that the workshop was hired to do. In this way, they could explore how their talents could best be used.

Apprentices were encouraged to study and copy other works of art as part of their training. Even other masters could be a source of new learning. Next door to Verrocchio's workshop, for example, was that of his rival, Antonio Pollaiuolo. Pollaiuolo's drawing *Ten Fighting Nudes* suggests that he might have been one of the first Renaissance artists to dissect corpses to study the human body. Da Vinci probably frequently visited Pollaiuolo's shop to see what kind of work was in progress.[5]

It was also common for skilled apprentices to add small details to the master's work, as training. Da Vinci's earliest known painting is of an angel and some landscaping in Verrocchio's work *Baptism of Christ*. This painting hints at the genius that da Vinci was to become. The delicate angel with curly blond hair seems to glow in a way that the rest of the painting does not.

Professions of the Renaissance

Before the Renaissance, the idea of rising to a higher social or economic class did not exist. Most people believed they were destined to live forever in the lifestyle into which they were born. Peasants remained peasants, nobles were always nobles. There was no middle class. That, people thought, was the will of God. But as the Renaissance bloomed, so too did the idea that every person had a right to choose his or her own destiny. As this idea grew, the opportunities for people to learn new professions and to rise in society through wealth and talent also grew.

Although there remained a distinct separation between the classes, the ideals of the Renaissance encompassed them all. Everyone was expected to know how to read and to do simple arithmetic. Even a lower-class laborer might have a good understanding of history, literature, and current events. Gradually, merchants and laborers, who had once been despised by the upper classes, became respected for their wealth and style.

Guilds

Once an apprentice had completed his training and showed a command of his craft, he could be admitted into a guild. Guilds were professional organizations that regulated the various crafts. They also made sure workers were treated fairly. Da Vinci and Verrocchio painted *Baptism of Christ* when da Vinci was about twenty, around the time da Vinci was accepted into the painter's guild of St. Luke's.

Each guild was made up of members of a trade, such as furriers, wool traders, or goldsmiths. The guild protected them from outside interferences of local government or the Roman Catholic Church. The system was very powerful. A member who broke a labor law would be brought before the mayor in the guildhall, instead of before the court of the monarch.[6] When an artist or craftsman was admitted to a guild, he was free to accept jobs from anyone. He could even open his own workshop if he wished.

Peasants

The lowest social class in every Renaissance town was the peasants. Today, the word *peasant* conjures up images of ragged, dirty people. This was not the case at all. During the Renaissance, a peasant was a farmer who grew food to sell in the city.

Although most land was owned by the wealthy, landowners usually lived in the cities rather than on their farms. Peasants ran the country farms in the absence of the owners in a crop-sharing relationship. They paid their masters a fee in exchange for having some claim to their crops.

In the countryside, proud peasant farmers might be in charge of hundreds of acres of farmland. Like farmers today, they raised pigs, chickens, sheep, and other animals to sell. Their fields might be planted with corn, vegetables, olive trees, and grapes for wine. In the off-seasons, many peasants spent a portion of their year working as artisans, innkeepers, fishermen, or sailors for extra income.

Although some peasants had good relationships with their masters, more often than not each feared and distrusted the other. One Renaissance writer, Leon Battista Alberti, clearly was not happy with the peasants he knew:

> The peasant . . . will ask for a loan to satisfy his creditors, to clothe his wife, to endow his daughters; then again he will ask you to pay for putting his cottage in order . . . then he will never stop complaining. . . . If the harvest is good he will keep the best share to himself. If, because of bad weather or some other reason the fields are barren this year the peasant will not let you have anything but the damage and losses.[7]

Laborers

The next class of people was made up of laborers. These working-class people, many of whom were poor, did most of the lower-paying jobs in the large cities. For example, in the textile industry there were silk weavers, spinners, and dyers. Hundreds of builders, blacksmiths, carpenters, sawyers, and wood-carvers toiled away in shipyards. Peddlers wandered city streets selling items from baskets on their backs. Shopkeepers sold everything from wine and ale to ribbons and thread. The romantic Venetian gondolier of today was, in Renaissance times, a laborer, similar to a modern taxi driver.

Many laborers were journeymen—former apprentices who had completed their training and had decided to strike out on their own. It was common for journeymen to gather in some public place at a certain time each day. Employers who needed workers would go there to find people to work for them. A laborer would be hired for as long as the job lasted, which could be from one day to many years. When the job was done, the laborer looked for more work.

Artists were considered laborers. In many cases, they were treated as such. Even da Vinci spent time working on commissions for a fee, such as designing costumes and floats for festivals and creating patterns for tapestries. Artists in powerful royal courts were viewed as the noble's personal servants. Artists gained respect and power through the patrons they managed to secure.

Different cities had laws governing when and where laborers could work. In Genoa, for example, workers in the wool industry worked from sunrise to sunset. They were forbidden to work after dark. They were allowed one meal break during the winter months, when the days were shorter, and two meal breaks during the longer summer days.[8] But workers did have some free time. No one worked on Sundays or on feast days. In some cities, such as Florence, workers had Saturday afternoon off.

Although the town laborers did most of the work, they were rarely respected for the jobs they did. Because laborers could work for many employers over the years, they had little control over how they were treated by those who hired them. It was common for employers to cheat workers out of their wages. Laborers often banded together and went on strike against the larger businesses that depended on them. They demanded more pay and better working conditions, just as labor unions sometimes do today.

The Middle Class

Although a town laborer's life might be difficult, he knew that, with a lot of work and some luck, he might become part of the wealthy, powerful middle class. The most common member of the new middle class was the entrepreneur—the businessperson who paid for the development of new inventions, who bought items low and sold high.[9]

During the Renaissance, the most money could be made through trade. Luxury goods such as silk, spices, pearls, fabrics, exotic woods, and gold were especially prized. Some merchants even grew rich enough to buy their own fleets of ships.

Professionals also made up a powerful part of the middle class. Bankers, lawyers, and doctors lived comfortable lives, much as they do today. Members of the powerful Medici family of Florence, for example, were successful bankers. The Medici Bank was one of the most powerful businesses in the Renaissance. It helped make the family rich. Da Vinci's father was a notary, which was considered a branch of the legal profession. He became a wealthy member of the middle class. Doctors served on many city councils alongside lawyers and other powerful leaders. The city of Padua, for instance, once paid a doctor two thousand ducats (Italian currency) a year to consult the people of the city on their medical problems. The city also let him continue to charge for his private practice.[10]

The Renaissance City-State

During the Renaissance, there was no such thing as "Italy." The area we know today as Italy was made up of independent cities and the surrounding areas called city-states. These city-states were, in many ways, like individual countries. They made their own laws, had their own money, and controlled their own armies. And like countries, they had their own personalities, strengths, and weaknesses.

Although there were dozens of city-states during the Renaissance, three rose to become the centers of power and culture. Venice was the center of trade and commerce for the world. Florence, dominated by the

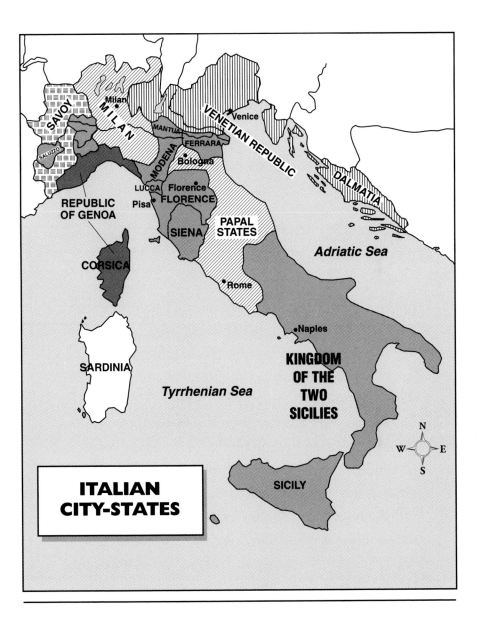

ITALIAN
CITY-STATES

*During the Renaissance, Italy as we know it today did not exist.
Instead, it was made up of many smaller city-states, including the
most famous—Venice, Florence, and Rome.*

powerful Medici family, was known as the heart of Renaissance art and culture. Rome, a forgotten city at the beginning of the Renaissance, lifted itself from the ruins of its past to become the focus for the new learning that marked the rise of the Renaissance throughout the world.

Venice, the City of Canals

With its famous canals, Venice is one of the best-known Italian cities today. Venice began as a small seaport. It quickly grew in importance during the Crusades. Venice soon became a major trade city, providing other cities with luxury goods from all over the world such as silks, spices, carpets and tapestries, gold and jewels, new foods, and slaves. European cities sent ships to Venice that were loaded with goods for the Eastern market, such as wool, wine, furs, and weapons.

Venice also became the center for the new printing trade, publishing one quarter of the world's books by the end of the fifteenth century.[11] Learned men from around the world settled in Venice, giving the city a reputation as a place of learning and culture. Even the art of Venice was something special. The city was renowned for the way light played in its streets and canals. Painters traveled to the famed city to try to capture this light in their art.

Venice hummed with life. In the main city square, called the piazza, moneylenders, bankers, shopkeepers, and goldsmiths set up rows of shops and booths.

Venice, famous for its system of canal transportation, is seen here as it looks today.

People streamed through the piazza, shopping and doing business. In the canals, ships from all over the world anchored side by side as workers unloaded barrels of wine, oil, food, rich fabrics, and caskets of spices.

Florence, the City of Flowers

Florence, or *Fiorenza*, means the city of flowers. This name perfectly described the colorful life of the city. Florence became known as the Renaissance city of learning, art, and beauty. It is also considered the world's first modern state.

Florence was a city where the ideas of individualism and personal freedom combined to form an open-minded, creative atmosphere that embraced new thinking in almost all areas. People felt free to express their opinions and to explore new ideas. As a result, new advances in art and science flowed from the city.

From its earliest days, Florence was run by a democratic government in which the guilds played a large role. To hold political office in Florence, a man had to be a member of a guild. Even the great author Dante had to join the druggist's guild just to become involved in city politics.[12] The greater guilds included the clothing and fabric manufacturers, fur merchants, physicians and druggists, and merchants. Members of these guilds were called *populo grasso* (fat or well-fed people). The lesser guilds included butchers, bakers, armorers, blacksmiths, carpenters, and innkeepers. Their members were called *populo minuto* (little people).

Florentine life was dominated by the powerful Medici family. This family's hold on Florence lasted for almost three hundred years. Its combination of wealth, power, and love of the arts turned Florence into the center for the greatest achievements in Renaissance art.

The Medicis

The founder of the Medici dynasty, Giovanni di Bicci de' Medici, founded the Medici Bank in 1397. Giovanni was a shrewd businessman. He gradually built his small business into a powerful money machine. The Medici Bank even loaned money to foreign royalty and to the city of Florence itself. When Giovanni died in 1429, his son Cosimo took over.

Cosimo de' Medici was as brilliant as his father. For more than thirty years, he continued to build the Medici Bank and opened branches in other cities. He was a powerful force in politics as well. He held offices and used his influence to control many areas of government. His skill at diplomacy won him the title "leading citizen," a powerful position in the government.

Cosimo's greatest contribution, however, was to learning and the arts. During his lifetime, he encouraged the new learning of the Renaissance. He was an avid rare-book collector. He funded the Platonic Academy, a center for Greek studies. He also encouraged artists and sculptors by commissioning great works.

However, Cosimo was outshone by his grandson, Lorenzo the Magnificent. Lorenzo was a ruthless politician, but he had a great love of the arts. His patronage of the arts brought Florence to the peak of Renaissance achievement. During Lorenzo's rule, da Vinci and fellow artist Sandro Botticelli painted in Florence. Lorenzo even fostered a young Michelangelo.

Lorenzo's death in 1492 marked the beginning of the decline of Florence and of the Renaissance itself. His son Piero, a weak leader, was eventually thrown

Lorenzo de' Medici, seen here in a portrait painted by artist Domenico Ghirlandaio, was perhaps the best-known patron of the Renaissance. His death would mark the beginning of the era's decline.

out of Florence when he failed to stop a French invasion. By the start of the sixteenth century, the Renaissance glory of Florence had begun to fade.

Rome, the City of Ruins

Rome, even during the Renaissance, was a city of ruins. The remains of the once-great Roman Empire lay scattered: crumbling buildings, broken streets, and forgotten artworks were buried beneath hundreds of years of neglect. One Renaissance witness sadly wrote, "the beauty of Rome is in ruins."[13] Cattle grazed in the ruins of the once-grand Roman Forum.

Slowly this began to change, starting with Pope Nicholas V, who led the Roman Catholic Church from 1447 to 1455. Nicholas V encouraged scholars to explore the forgotten libraries and to save the ancient texts. He used church money to repair old buildings and erect new ones. He loaned money to Roman citizens who renovated much of the city. He was also one of the greatest patrons of the arts.

Nicholas began a process of rebuilding Rome that peaked when Julius II became Pope in 1503. For more than fifty years, church leaders encouraged the new learning. They embraced the arts by commissioning works to decorate religious buildings in Rome and in all the city-states.

Eventually, however, wars and political unrest took the place of the arts and learning. By the late 1500s, the new Rome had faded. Although Rome continued to be an important cultural center, it never again rose to the glory that it had once seen during the height of the Renaissance.

Although little is known about da Vinci's life as an apprentice, it is easy to imagine what kind of impression that city life made on a young man from the country. By the time the teenage da Vinci marveled at the sights and sounds of Florence, life in any of the great Italian cities, and life in the Renaissance, was full of excitement and adventure.

Chapter 4

Beauty in a Beautiful World

The painter contends with and rivals nature.

—Leonardo da Vinci [1]

By the time da Vinci was in his mid-twenties, he had left his apprenticeship and begun his career as a professional artist. It was the start of one of the most celebrated art careers that the Renaissance—or any other age—has ever seen.

To understand why da Vinci became the great artist that he was, it is important to know what came before him. Art before the Renaissance consisted mainly of two-dimensional images painted on flat backgrounds. There was little attempt to show depth or emotion. It was considered bad taste, even sinful, to celebrate the common man through art.

By da Vinci's time, attitudes had changed. People began to appreciate humanity and all its facets. Artists

Da Vinci's talent lay partly in his ability to capture human emotion in his work.

began exploring the idea of using everyday scenes and objects in art. Every day it seemed that some new idea about depth, color, or perspective was discovered.

Da Vinci was brilliant. He was able to combine his great artistic talent with the new ideas about painting to create art like nothing people had ever seen before. He could capture a moment of human emotion that gave his paintings a depth that was not felt elsewhere.

Da Vinci spent hours, even days, wandering through the countryside. His paintings are filled with details of the natural world. Few artists had brought so much of the natural world into their art. When da Vinci did it, it was extraordinary. For example, da

Source Document

These beasts always go in troops, and the oldest goes in front and the second in age remains the last, and thus they enclose the troop. . . . The females do not fight as with other animals; and it is so merciful that it is unwilling by nature ever to hurt those weaker than itself. And if it meets in the middle of its way a flock of sheep it puts them aside with its trunk, so as not to trample them under foot. . . . [2]

Leonardo da Vinci studied animals and people almost every day, writing down everything he noticed for future reference. Here, he describes in his notebooks some of the behavior of elephants.

Vinci's angels have exquisite three-dimensional wings. It is clear that he spent much time studying birds, for every feather can be seen in delicate detail.

Da Vinci's almost obsessive interest in anatomy also appears in his work. To study human faces, for example, da Vinci spent hours following strangers on the street, sketching them for future paintings. He tirelessly sketched hundreds of images of the human body. He also observed animals such as cats, horses, birds, insects, and anything else that caught his imagination. Everything he discovered, he used in his art.

Da Vinci's Art

Da Vinci's reputation as one of the world's greatest artists rests on less than fifteen known works. More surprising still, he left most of his works unfinished for reasons that still baffle historians. Biographer Giorgio Vasari gave a possible reason for this. He wrote of da Vinci, "the instability of his character caused him to take up and abandon many things."[3]

It is possible that da Vinci left some of his paintings unfinished because his quick, easily bored mind turned to other things. In a letter to the famous Renaissance woman Isabella d'Este, a frustrated friend named Pietro da Novellara wrote, "Leonardo's life is changeful and uncertain; it is thought that he lives only for the day. . . . The sketch is not yet complete. . . . He is entirely wrapped up in geometry and has no patience for painting."[4] Most agree that da Vinci was incapable of finishing anything. Vasari wrote, "For his many admirable qualities, with which he was so richly endowed, although he talked of more things than he actually accomplished, his fame can never be extinguished."[5]

Although all of da Vinci's paintings are significant, a few stand out for their beauty and power. Some are unfinished, others are complete, but they all highlight both his life and the Renaissance as a time of new discoveries in all aspects of life.

The Adoration of the Magi

In 1481, when da Vinci was twenty-nine, he was hired to paint the altarpiece, or screen behind the altar, for the Church of San Donato Scopeto outside Florence. Da Vinci made many studies, or sketches, of this painting before he began it. However, he never completed the work.

The picture now hangs in the Uffizi museum in Florence. It shows a group of people crowded around a seated Madonna holding the Christ Child. In the background are riders on horseback. The horses are drawn so powerfully that they seem to move. Each face in the picture is distinctive, with its own personality and emotion. Although it is unfinished, the painting hints at the glory that might have been.

Benois Madonna

This painting, now in the Hermitage Museum in Russia, is in very poor condition. Heavy varnish clouds the colors of the painting. The varnish is so dark that the Madonna's teeth are hidden, making her look toothless.

The *Benois Madonna* was discovered by scholars in a private art collection in 1909. There is no information about what had happened to it before then. As soon as art experts saw the fresh beauty of the *Madonna* and the style of the painting's composition, they were convinced that it was the work of da Vinci. Da Vinci chose to paint a simple everyday scene of a young mother delighted with her new baby. She smiles at her child, who sits on her lap. The baby, curious about a flower, gently reaches for it. It is a simple, quiet scene, which makes it all the more powerful.

No one had ever painted a religious subject in an everyday setting before da Vinci's *Madonna*. From that moment on, artists began to show religious scenes more personally. They used the beauty and power of everyday life to represent the glory of God.

Virgin of the Rocks

In 1483, da Vinci was commissioned to decorate an ancona for the Church of San Francesco Grande in Milan. An ancona is a wooden altar that has frames into which paintings are inserted. Da Vinci's job was to paint the Virgin Mary for the center panel. There are two versions of this painting. One is in the Louvre Museum in Paris and the other is in the National Gallery in London. Scholars feel that the two canvases are two versions of the same painting, with some variations.[6]

Virgin of the Rocks *is one of da Vinci's most famous works.*

The scene shows four figures: the Madonna, an angel, and two infants. One baby is the Christ Child. The other is John the Baptist. The figures are seated beside a pool of water in a cavelike grotto. In the painting, da Vinci took advantage of his ideas of showing the natural world in art. Instead of picturing the holy family on thrones or wearing rich garments, da Vinci chose to put them in a quiet, natural place. The Virgin Mary is a radiant beauty whose only concern is the happiness of her baby.

Mona Lisa

The smile. The eyes. The *Mona Lisa* is unquestionably the most famous painting in the world. It was even famous during da Vinci's lifetime. Biographer Vasari wrote, "whoever desires to see how far art can imitate nature, may do so by observing this head."[7]

Da Vinci painted the portrait on wood in about 1503, near the end of his life. No one is sure who the woman is. Some suggest that it was the wife of Francesco del Giocondo, a Florentine nobleman. It is one of the few paintings da Vinci completed. For unknown reasons, he kept it after it was finished. When he died, his friend and patron Francis I, the king of France, acquired it.

It remained the property of French royalty for centuries. It even hung in the royal bathroom. In 1801, the royal art collection became the foundation for the famous Louvre Museum. The *Mona Lisa* was one of its most prized pieces.

It remained there until Tuesday, August 22, 1911. On that day, while security guards were away, someone walked into the museum, took the *Mona Lisa* from the wall, and simply walked out the door. The most famous painting in the world had been stolen.

The world was in an uproar. It seemed as if the *Mona Lisa* had disappeared forever. Finally, more than two years after it was stolen, a Florentine antique dealer named Alfredo Geri received a letter from a man claiming to have the painting. The dealer agreed to meet with the man and immediately contacted the police. The next day, Geri and an art expert, Giovanni Poggi, went to the man's hotel room.

The men gathered inside the stranger's hotel room as police surrounded the building. Geri was astounded when the man reached into a clothes trunk and "lifted up the false bottom of the trunk, under which we saw the picture. . . . It was indeed the authentic work of Leonardo da Vinci. The smile of the *Mona Lisa* was again alive in Florence."[8]

The thief, a house painter named Vincenzo Peruggia, had once worked in the Louvre. He had vowed to return all of the Italian paintings in the Louvre to their "rightful" home in Italy. The *Mona Lisa* was the first one to go. When he was asked why he chose it, he replied that it had seemed to him the most beautiful. Eventually, the painting was returned to the Louvre.

The *Mona Lisa* has been so famous for so long that it is sometimes difficult to see what the fuss is all

Da Vinci's Mona Lisa *has become one of the most famous and loved paintings not only of the Renaissance, but of all time.*

about. But if the painting is seen not as a cultural icon but as a great work of art, it becomes easier to see why a French scholar would say of it, "I have never seen anything more finished or expressive. There is so much grace and so much sweetness in the eyes and the features of the face that it seems alive."[9]

The Masterpiece That Never Was: Da Vinci's Bronze Horse

Da Vinci always loved a challenge. In 1489, he was presented with a huge one. That year, he was asked to produce an enormous bronze statue of a horse for the Sforza family. No one had ever created a statue such as the one da Vinci was asked to do. It was a challenge the artist could not refuse.

Da Vinci set out to tackle the problems head on. He sketched hundreds of horses in dozens of positions. He measured their proportions, their bone and muscle structure, and the movement of their limbs.[10] He devoted entire sections of his notebooks to model building, preparing molds, and casting metal. He invented new ways for casting bronze that had never been tried before. No detail was too small for da Vinci to consider.

By 1493, da Vinci had constructed a breathtaking life-size clay model for the statue. The twenty-three-foot-high statue was so impressive that it was officially unveiled during the betrothal celebrations of Bianca Marie Sforza, the daughter of one of da Vinci's wealthy patrons.[11]

Da Vinci drew these sketches as part of his preparation for the design of the Sforza family's bronze horse monument.

Unfortunately, world events worked against da Vinci and his great horse. In 1499, French troops invaded Milan, where the statue was being made. Da Vinci fled to Venice. French troops used the enormous earthen model for target practice, and all traces of the great statue disappeared.

Other Great Artists of the Renaissance

Da Vinci was not the only artist to produce great Renaissance art. Others, many just as famous as da Vinci during their lifetimes, left a legacy of great art and beauty. The Renaissance belonged to them as well, and their work remains some of the greatest art to come out of the Renaissance period.

Sandro Botticelli

The painter Sandro Botticelli, who was born in 1445, worked alongside a young da Vinci in Verrocchio's workshop as a fellow apprentice. Botticelli, like da Vinci, studied science and anatomy to make his paintings more realistic. But eventually, he chose to paint mythological and fantastical subjects.

Botticelli's most famous painting is called the *Birth of Venus*. In this painting, Venus, the Roman goddess of love and beauty, rises from the foamy ocean waves upon a large cockleshell. This painting has the dreamy quality for which Botticelli was known.

Although he was well-known and well-respected as an artist, he was also considered somewhat eccentric. According to Vasari, "He is said to have made a great deal of money and to have spent it all, being a very bad manager. Finally, very old and unfit for work, he went about on crutches and so died in his sixty-seventh year after long illness and decrepitude."[12]

Michelangelo Buonarroti

Michelangelo is perhaps second only to da Vinci in fame as a Renaissance master. Michelangelo was born in Milan in 1475, about the time that da Vinci was striking out on his own as a painter. Michelangelo's strong personality and brilliant artistic talent was unrivaled during the Renaissance. Even da Vinci felt the competition.

Michelangelo's David *is often considered the perfect male form. It has become one of the most famous examples of Renaissance sculpture.*

Michelangelo was a sculptor, not a painter, and his sculptures are considered some of the greatest artworks in the world. His most famous statue is the eighteen-foot-tall *David*. Michelangelo astounded the world with his statue of the courageous David, who stands keen-eyed and ready to face Goliath.

After a long and celebrated life, Michelangelo died on February 17, 1564. Vasari described his funeral, saying,

> All the painters, sculptors, and architects assembled quietly. . . . At nightfall they gathered silently around the corpse. The oldest and most distinguished masters each took a torch, while the younger artists at the same moment raised the bier [frame that a corpse is laid on]. . . . All desired the glory of having borne to earth the remains of the greatest man ever known to the arts.[13]

The Sistine Chapel

In 1508, Michelangelo was asked to paint the ceiling of the Sistine Chapel in Rome. At first, he declined. He said he was a sculptor, not a painter. But Pope Sixtus IV pressured him, and he finally agreed. For four years, Michelangelo labored, painting while lying on his back, in poor light, with paint dripping on his face.

The completed ceiling is a thing of astonishment. Michelangelo's masterpiece is a symphony of color and movement. Hundreds of figures, depicting scenes from the Old Testament, swirl together. Even during his lifetime, the world was astounded by Michelangelo's vision. Vasari wrote, "Everyone capable of judging stands amazed at the excellence of this work, at the grace and flexibility. . . . All the world hastened to behold this marvel and was overwhelmed, speechless with astonishment."[14] People from around the world traveled to Rome just to see the magnificent ceiling.

Over the centuries, as the painting aged, the ceiling grew dull and discolored. Many attempts at restoration were made. At some point, clothing was painted over nude figures. A massive cleaning project began in the 1980s. Art experts gently wiped away centuries of grime with a special cleaning fluid that would not harm the paint. They were even able to remove some of the overpainting that had been done centuries after the ceiling was completed.

The work was finished in 1990. What emerged astounded even the loudest critics. The cleaned ceiling pulses with life. Michelangelo's colors, always bright and clear, now shone with a new light. Today, the ceiling of the Sistine Chapel resonates the way it was intended. It glorifies both the Renaissance and the artist whose vision and skill created it.

Raffaello Sanzio, or Raphael

Considered part of the trio of Renaissance masters, along with da Vinci and Michelangelo, Raphael was born in Urbino in 1483. Raphael's talent was so great that, when he was twenty-five, he was called to Rome by Pope Julius II to decorate the state rooms in the Vatican. When he arrived, Michelangelo was already working on the Sistine Chapel.

Raphael's work, although not as revolutionary as Leonardo da Vinci's or Michelangelo's, had a spectacular quality all its own: "In his art, individuals move with dignity and grace through a calm, intelligible, and ordered world."[15] One of Raphael's best-known works is a painting called *School of Athens*. In this painting, a large group of scholars and philosophers from history have gathered in an airy room decorated with statues of Greek figures. The men are grouped around the room, clearly involved in discussions and debates. The great Greek philosophers Plato and Aristotle stand in the center. Other famous Greek thinkers, including Pythagoras and Ptolemy, surround them.

In their midst sits a man, his chin resting on his hand. It is believed that this figure is a portrait of Michelangelo, which Raphael added as he was completing the painting. This figure shows a mass and power not to be found elsewhere in the painting.[16]

Raphael went on to become famous and was showered with commissions for the rest of his life. Sadly, he died at age thirty-seven after a brief illness. The world would never know what greatness Raphael might have reached had he lived.

Tiziano Vecelli, or Titian

Like da Vinci, Titian's early years are not well-known. He was probably born around 1488. Although scholars still debate Titian's early life, his documented career spans about sixty-eight years.

Titian, considered one of the most brilliant of the painters of the Renaissance, did this portrait titled La Flora.

Titian is credited with discovering a type of brushwork that layered colors one on top of the other, creating a depth of light and color that was very new at the time. His portraits of Renaissance citizens, from the Pope on down, capture their personalities in a way that no one had ever managed before. Likewise, his nudes glow with healthy color.

One of his most famous paintings is *Venus of Urbino*. This nude woman, reclining seductively on a rich couch, calmly gazes out at the viewer. Venus's body has a creamy glow. A small dog sleeps at her feet. There is a calmness, almost a sleepiness, to the painting. Titian painted many reclining nudes after *Venus of Urbino*, but this particular painting created an image and style that has been imitated by artists ever since.

Almost four hundred surviving paintings are attributed to this great Renaissance master, who lived to be eighty-eight years old. Today, Titian is considered one of the most brilliant painters to emerge during the Renaissance.

Unlike Titian, da Vinci, the best-known artist of the Renaissance, did not leave hundreds of works behind. Although da Vinci's legacy of paintings is small, however, his works have influenced artists for more than four hundred years. Most of the great Renaissance painters created their most famous works in the years after da Vinci's death. These artists rode the wave of artistic freedom that da Vinci helped create.

Knowledge Is Power

*My subjects require for their expression
not the words of others but experience.*

—Leonardo da Vinci[1]

Throughout his adult life, da Vinci filled page after page with his thoughts, observations, and drawings. These writings, gathered together in notebooks, form the most comprehensive surviving account of da Vinci's work. It is through these writings that Leonardo da Vinci's brilliance as a scholar and as a part of the Renaissance shines.

Da Vinci's Notebooks

When da Vinci was about thirty years old, he began recording his thoughts in notebooks that he carried wherever he went. Whatever was occupying his mind at any given time made its way into these notebooks. When da Vinci was fascinated with the properties of water, for example, he filled a notebook with observations and theories about its properties. Another notebook includes anatomical drawings and details of the human body. Still another notebook includes military machines and ideas that were so far ahead of their time that it would take centuries for the world to rediscover the concepts that da Vinci had thought of hundreds of years before.

The most striking part of da Vinci's notebooks is his handwriting. Da Vinci's elegant, spidery handwriting is written left-handed and backward. The only way to read his writing is through a mirror. Some scholars believe he wrote this way because he was trying to encode his ideas. Others maintain that it was simply easier for the left-handed da Vinci to write backward. No one will ever know for sure. But da Vinci's unique writing style is one of the elements of his life that gives him an air of brilliance and mystery.

The notebooks are a treasure trove of information about da Vinci as a painter, inventor, and theorist, but strangely, they contain little personal information. Some scholars have said that da Vinci's notebooks are more like an encyclopedia than a diary. This is very true. He rarely recorded personal information or his feelings. Occasionally, however, there is a glimpse of da Vinci, the man, in the notebooks. At the bottom of one page there is an unexpected list: "Tuesday: bread, meat, wine, fruit, minestra, salad."[2] Was this a grocery list? A menu? There is no way to tell. But these everyday words, scribbled among lofty ideas about

Source Document

Leonardo da Vinci's notebooks show his unique handwriting, which was done not only left-handed, but also backward.

mathematics, art, and science, give a glimpse into the life of the Renaissance and da Vinci.

The World of Humanism

Although da Vinci had a habit of recording everything he observed, he was not the only one who was inspired by the freedom of thought that came with the Renaissance. The era was filled with new thinking in literature, philosophy, art, religion, and medicine.

However, the "new" knowledge that people craved was really very old. Two hundred years before da Vinci, people were rediscovering the past that had been so long neglected. In 1392, one writer praised history as the "true creator of man," saying that humanity consists of the memory of past actions in the world today.[3] Slowly, as writings of ancient Rome and Greece came to light, scholars began to realize how much information had been neglected. Much of the information had been repressed by the Catholic Church, which maintained that any beliefs that did not conform with Christianity should be destroyed.

The rediscovery of the "new learning" came along with the idea that an individual could control his or her own destiny. This idea, called humanism, emphasized individual conduct and the pursuit of the good of the people: "The proper study of mankind was now to be man, in all the potential strength and beauty of his body, in all the joy and pain of his senses and feelings, in all the frail majesty of his reason."[4]

For the first time, individuals could choose their own destinies and pursue their own interests. The Renaissance was, above all, the time of "many-sided men."[5] Merchants and statesmen were often fluent in many languages, including Greek. Everyone, from the loftiest noble to the lowliest laborer, could learn to read. There was no limit to what someone could do.

Humanism and the Catholic Church

As humanism spread, the Roman Catholic Church struggled with how to handle the new thinking. For centuries, the church held that the only way for humans to be moral was to follow the teachings of Jesus Christ. Every aspect of an individual's life was believed to be part of a master plan. Everyone was given his or her situation in life by God, and it would be against God to change it.

Humanism changed all that. It seemed, at first, a dangerous idea to the Catholic Church. Paul II, who became Pope in 1464, proclaimed that "pagan" learning should be outlawed.[6] Most Renaissance humanists, however, did not renounce their belief in God and the Catholic Church. They combined their beliefs in God with the idea that people could use their talents and ideas to glorify God and all of mankind. By the time da Vinci was born, the Catholic Church had accepted humanism as well. It funded the massive city projects and public artworks that enabled humanist artists to use their skills to glorify God in art, sculpture, and architecture.

Written Works of the Renaissance

Just as the Renaissance was a time of great works of fine art, it was also a time of great literature. The ideas of humanism joined with a new acceptance of a person's ability—and right—to think and dream. This heady combination resulted in some of the most important written works that the world has ever seen.

Dante's *Divine Comedy*

Dante's masterpiece was written in the early 1300s, almost a hundred years before the peak of the Renaissance. But it helped pave the way for a literary revolution that would sweep all of Europe by the end of the 1500s.

Dante Alighieri was a Florentine nobleman who, in 1302, was banished from his beloved Florence for supporting the losing side in an ongoing political struggle. For years, he wandered. During this time, he wrote a poem he called *Commedia*. Far from being a humorous story, this poem, called *The Divine Comedy* today, is the tale of a man's journey through hell in search of paradise. But it was more than a good story. With it, "Dante almost single-handedly invented the Italian language."[7]

Before Dante, most works were written in Latin, the language of scholars and the Roman Catholic Church. Few others could read and write Latin. The majority of people who could read at all learned the language and dialect of the regions where they lived. Dante wrote in the Tuscan dialect of Florence and combined it with Latin words and phrases to create a lyrical, unique book. His language became the language of the people, and eventually, of Italy itself.

The Divine Comedy had such a far-reaching influence that, more than one hundred fifty years after its publication, it is said that Leonardo da Vinci and Michelangelo got into an argument over it. It seems that a group of men were in a piazza in Florence discussing the poem when da Vinci passed by. Knowing that da Vinci was knowledgeable about Dante, they asked for his thoughts. Just at that moment, Michelangelo appeared. Da Vinci is said to have exclaimed, "Here is Michelangelo, he will explain the verses." The sculptor, many years younger than da Vinci, thought the old master was making fun of him and replied, "Explain them yourself! You who made the model of a horse to be cast in bronze and could not cast it and left it unfinished, to your shame!" Da Vinci blushed, embarrassed, as the furious Michelangelo stomped away.[8]

The *Decameron*

The Decameron was an early Renaissance work that, like *The Divine Comedy*, influenced world literature and Renaissance writings for generations after it was published. *The Decameron* was written by Florentine writer and humanist Giovanni Boccaccio. Born the illegitimate son of a merchant, Boccaccio grew to be a respected Renaissance thinker. He published a number of scholarly works before he wrote *The*

Decameron, which he dismissed as not particularly good.

The Decameron (Ten Days' Work) is a collection of a hundred witty, intelligent stories told by ten people—seven women and three men—who flee an outbreak of the plague and take refuge in a country villa outside the city. To amuse themselves during the ten days that they are in the country, they entertain one another with stories. The book is known not only for its poetry and rich language but also for its descriptions of daily life and how people dealt with the horrors of the plague. Although Boccaccio went on to write more works, *The Decameron* is his most famous. The framework of the book has been copied by authors ever since.

Machiavelli's *The Prince*

Perhaps no other Renaissance writer influenced both literature and society as Niccolò Machiavelli did with his book *The Prince*, one of the most controversial works of the entire Italian Renaissance. Machiavelli, the son of a Florentine lawyer, grew up in a modest middle-class family. As an adult, he was swept up in Florentine politics. Eventually, he was cast from his political position, accused as a traitor, and tortured. After his release, he went into a self-imposed exile in the Florentine countryside to escape his enemies. There, he wrote *The Prince*.

Machiavelli, perhaps remembering what he went through in the political world, argued that rulers

Source Document

Upon this a question arises: whether it be better to be loved than feared or feared than loved? It may be answered that one should wish to be both, but, because it is difficult to unite them in one person, it is much safer to be feared than loved, when, of the two, either must be dispensed with. Because this is to be asserted in general of men, that they are ungrateful, fickle, false, cowardly, covetous, and as long as you succeed they are yours entirely; they will offer you their blood, property, life, and children . . . when the need is far distant; but when it approaches they turn against you. And that prince who, relying entirely on their promises, has neglected other precautions, is ruined; because friendships that are obtained by payments, and not by greatness or nobility of mind, may indeed be earned, but they are not secured, and in time of need cannot be relied upon. . . .[9]

Machiavelli's political masterpiece, The Prince, *is still considered by some a model for how leaders should govern their people.*

should rule with power and cunning rather than with virtue and kindness. According to *The Prince*, all men are by nature cruel and corrupt. Machiavelli wrote, "Whoever wishes to found a state and give it laws must start with assuming that all men are bad."[10] In *The Prince*, any action, however amoral, could be excused if it resulted in a stable government.

Although *The Prince* was controversial during the Renaissance, it was not until after Machiavelli's death that the work became well-known. Ever since its publication, Machiavelli's ideas have been hotly debated. *The Prince* was even responsible for a new word in the English language: *Machiavellian*, which means deceptive and dishonest.

Gutenberg and Movable Type

Until the Renaissance, books were painstakingly created by hand, one at a time. Large cities had hordes of professional copiers. These people were hired to reproduce popular works, usually by scholars or wealthy patrons who could afford their services. Other than a few important works, such as the Bible, most writings were confined to only a few copies each, which were circulated among small groups of people.

In the mid-1400s, a new invention changed all that—movable type. The art of printing came fully formed into the world at the precise moment that it was most needed.[11] It gave the ideas of the Renaissance a form in which they could spread all over the world.

The credit for the invention of printing goes to a German goldsmith named Johannes Gutenberg. Gutenberg was the first person to patent the idea of melting and molding metal into letters that could be rearranged to form different words. For the first time, books could be created in days instead of years. But more importantly, books could be mass-produced—ensuring that anyone with the ability to read and a little money could have access to the knowledge that was once reserved for the wealthy and the Catholic Church.

By 1450, Gutenberg began using his printing press commercially. Sometime around 1452, he borrowed money to start his new business. However, he was unable to repay the loan. By 1455, his creditors took everything. Gutenberg died in 1468, almost penniless. But he had begun a revolution that would change the world.

By 1465, printing had come to Italy. Within five more years, there was a press in France.[12] With the explosion of printing came a hunger for books, which this new industry was more than happy to provide. In just a few years, professional print shops throughout Europe were producing books at a rapid rate.

Although Gutenberg did not live to see the far-reaching results of his invention, he did leave the world a priceless legacy. In 1455, just before he lost everything, his workshop created a number of large Bibles. These works, today called Gutenberg Bibles, are masterful works of beauty. These Bibles are the

Source Document

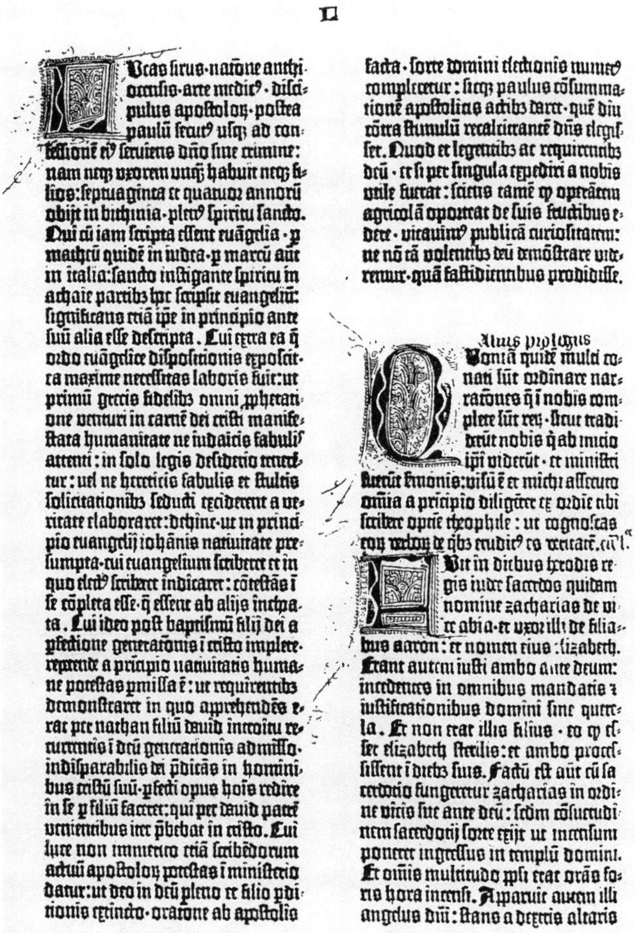

Johannes Gutenberg left a permanent mark on the world with his invention of movable type, which, for the first time, helped bring reasonably priced books to ordinary people. This is a page from an original Gutenberg Bible.

only objects known to have been printed by Gutenberg himself. They represent the first step in what became one of the Renaissance's greatest achievements.

Da Vinci reaped the rewards of all these kinds of "new thinking" throughout his life. The ideas gave him, and many others, the freedom to change the world.

Chapter 6

A World of New Ideas

*To obtain an exact and complete knowledge,
I have dissected more than ten human bodies.*

—Leonardo da Vinci [1]

In page after page of da Vinci's notebooks are sketches and drawings of every conceivable part of the human body—from teeth and muscles to the stomach and the heart. On one page there is a tiny fetus, curled with its head between its knees, surrounded by a cutaway view of the mother's womb. The skeleton of a hand, with each bone numbered, slides down from the top of another page.

Da Vinci was one of the first artists to realize that, to be a good artist, one had to understand nature. With his brilliant mind and the ability to draw quickly and accurately, da Vinci set about to study and record as much of the natural world as he could. The

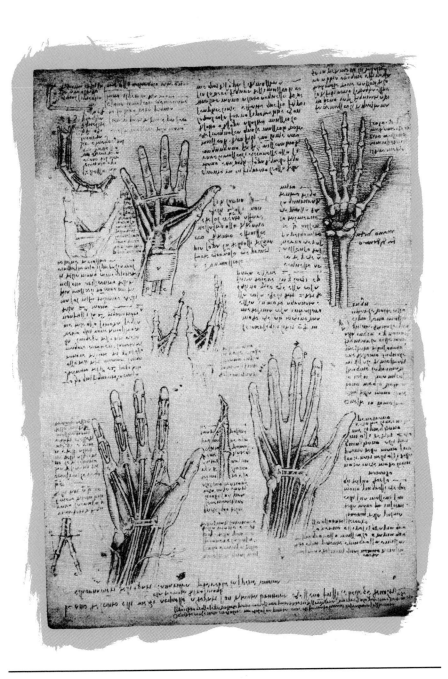

Leonardo da Vinci was remarkable for his extremely detailed studies of every aspect of the human body, from the organs to the bones.

freshness and originality of da Vinci's scientific drawings are still evident today, more than four hundred years after he carefully created them. Part of the reason for this is that da Vinci was a master observer *and* a master artist. His hands, eyes, and brain were coordinated through self-training. He was gradually able to turn himself into a living, breathing camera.[2]

Another reason that da Vinci's drawings are so lifelike is that he studied the human body firsthand, by dissecting dead bodies. At that time, most scholars relied on animal dissections and ancient texts for information. Da Vinci, however, wanted to discover the secrets of the human body for himself. Da Vinci's first biographer, Paolo Giovi, wrote,

> in the medical faculty he learned to dissect the cadavers of criminals under inhuman, disgusting conditions . . . because he wanted to examine and to draw the different deflections and reflections of limbs and their dependence upon the nerves and the joints. This is why he paid attention to the forms of even very small organs, capillaries and hidden parts of the skeleton.[3]

But it was more than an interest in accuracy that spurred da Vinci. As the Renaissance moved forward, a new philosophy took hold, based on firsthand observation and experiments on nature.[4] Da Vinci believed, as did other Renaissance thinkers, that answers could be found by observation and study. With the thirst for new knowledge, people of the Renaissance wanted to know for themselves how the natural world worked.

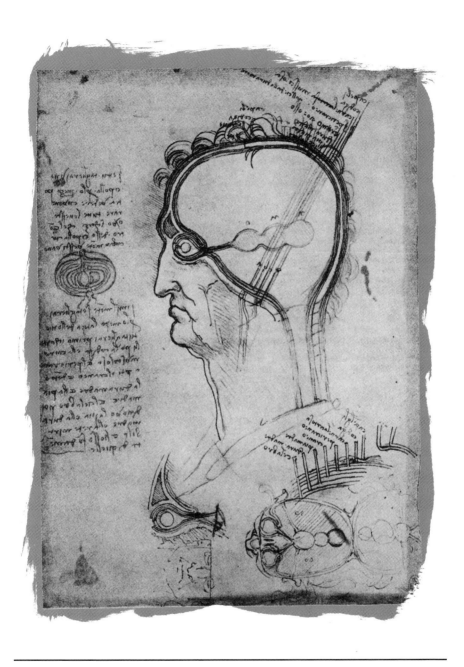

Da Vinci gained most of his knowledge about the human body by dissecting corpses to study the inner workings of the body.

They set out on a quest of discovery in all aspects of the world around them.

Astronomy and Navigation

The year that da Vinci celebrated his fortieth birthday, another Italian, Christopher Columbus, landed on the shores of the New World for the first time. This amazing feat could not have been accomplished during any other time but the Renaissance, when scientists and scholars studying mathematics, astronomy, and navigation made incredible advances.

Long ago, most people believed that the earth was flat. Ancient Greeks such as Ptolemy had been convinced that the earth was round. Some medieval scholars who were familiar with their work agreed. Ptolemy and most of his followers did not believe that, if a ship sailed to the west, it would tumble over the edge of the earth.[5] However, during the Middle Ages, there was no way to test the ancient theories. Early ships traveled slowly, hugging the shore. No one knew what lay past the horizon. The idea that the world was flat was a terrifying possibility.

During the Renaissance, the flat-earth theory was challenged by many scholars. Ptolemy's ideas about astronomy and the position of the stars were looked at in a new way. Scientists realized that they could use Ptolemy's theories not only to calculate the size of the earth, but also to pinpoint a ship's position on a huge sea. However, just reading Ptolemy's classic astronomical text was not enough. The goal was the revival of the ancient practice of astronomy.[6]

Renaissance astronomers such as Johannes Müller, who was known as Regiomontanus, and Georg von Peuerbach designed instruments such as the quadrant, which measures the altitude of the sun and the stars. They also built observatories to study the sky. Other inventions, such as the compass and the astrolabe (a device used to measure the position of a star) made long sea voyages possible. In 1490, the known world was still limited to what Ptolemy had known more than twelve hundred years earlier. By 1521, however, a ship had sailed on every ocean around the globe.[7]

Another Renaissance astronomer, Nicolaus Copernicus, pondered an astronomical problem that had vexed scholars for centuries: Did Earth revolve around the sun, or was Earth the center of the universe? For more than thirty years, he struggled with the problem. The telescope had not been invented yet, and no instruments at the time could prove his theories. Instead, he used mathematics to determine that Earth must move around the sun.

But the idea that caused the most laughter was Copernicus's belief that Earth itself revolved. Scholars of the day scoffed. Of course Earth was not moving, they said. If it did, then birds would be left behind, a falling stone would never reach the ground, and the air would be whisked off the globe![8] It was not until the early 1600s, when the telescope was invented, that many of Copernicus's theories were verified by another great Italian astronomer, Galileo Galilei.

Medicine

Like astronomy, medicine also made great strides during the Renaissance. Until that time, healing the sick was not a profession. In the Middle Ages, a knowledge of medical theory and a basic skill in treating the common accidents and ailments of life was regarded as essential for ordinary life.[9]

During the Renaissance, however, medicine began to be seen as a vital study, worthy of professional status. Many cities began licensing their physicians, and becoming a doctor was a viable career. But doctors of the Renaissance were completely unlike doctors today. A university-trained physician, considered the expert, diagnosed an ailment. Below physicians were surgeons, who actually performed procedures on patients. Apothecaries, who were experts on drugs and herbs for healing, came below surgeons.

The biggest achievement in medicine during the Renaissance came with the organization of the profession and the growing acceptance of medicine as a worthy art. In Venice, for example, physicians were required by law to meet once a month to exchange information and to take classes in anatomy once a year.[10] Other laws regulated how much apothecaries could charge for drugs and prohibited physicians from practicing without a degree.

The greatest medical advancements came through the study of human anatomy by dissection. In the early days of the Renaissance, the Roman Catholic Church frowned on dissection, mainly due to superstition and fear, combined with the very real possibility of the spread of disease. But by the time that da Vinci was engrossed in his studies of the human body in the late 1400s, dissection was officially authorized by the church.

One of the greatest scholars in this field was Andreas Vesalius. In 1543, he published a work called *On the Structure of the Human Body*. This book provided the foundation for modern medicine and anatomy. It was also a landmark in printing.[11] In his book, Vesalius corrected many errors that ancient scholars had made and included detailed illustrations of the human body. Although he did make some errors, his work would be used by students for generations afterward.

Botany

Botany, the study of plants, has been a vital part of medicine for centuries. Most drugs came from herbs and plants. Botany served a practical and immediate purpose, placing in the hands of the physician an increasing number of medicinal herbs.[12] As the Renaissance opened up new ideas in science, botany became a new and exciting area of study. But not only was the study of botany good for medicine, it was also considered a way to better understand the world and to delight in the beauty of plants for their own sake.

The first botanical gardens were in Italy, usually grown by wealthy families such as the Medicis. The Medici gardens were known for their exquisite beauty, with countless specimens of different trees and shrubs.[13] Other villas throughout Italy boasted lush gardens filled with roses, fruit trees, and plants, and herb gardens filled with medicinal plants.

But it was the invention of the printing press that turned botany into a widespread science. At the time, there was no accurate way to describe plants technically. Most scientists relied on detailed illustrations for study. With the advent of printing, entire books filled

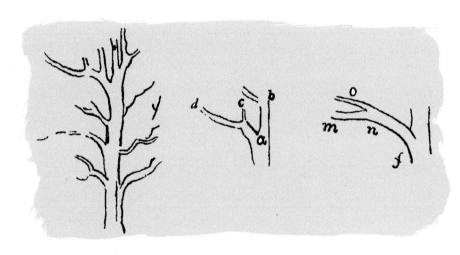

Da Vinci, like some other Renaissance thinkers of his time, studied almost every conceivable topic. Here, in his notebooks, he drew diagrams indicating his study of botany, which he did to give him better perspective for his paintings.

with botanical illustrations could, for the first time, be used by scientists all over the world.

Da Vinci's Bicycle

In 1966, monks restoring a recently rediscovered da Vinci manuscript made a startling discovery. On the inside of a page that had been folded and glued together for more than four hundred years, they found a crude drawing of what is unmistakably a bicycle. Scholars were stunned. Here was evidence that the great da Vinci had imagined a two-wheeled vehicle more than three hundred years before it was invented.

The drawing is of a remarkably modern-looking bicycle. It has T-shaped handlebars, pedals, and a gear-and-chain system. A saddle rises above the rear wheel and is attached by a bar. Scholars believe that the sketches—including the bicycle—may have been drawn by one of da Vinci's apprentices. The drawings are too crude to be from the hand of the master. The drawing is most likely a copy of something da Vinci drew himself.

But is the sketch proof that da Vinci invented the bicycle? The debate has raged ever since the mysterious drawing was discovered. Some believe that the drawing is authentic, arguing the fact that it was hidden for centuries. They point to an authentic da Vinci drawing of a toothed gear-and-chain system similar to what was used on modern bicycles as evidence that he could have envisioned a bicycle.

Others insist that the drawing is a fake, sketched by one of the monks in an attempt to make da Vinci appear even more brilliant. Their evidence includes the fact that the brown crayon markings of the bicycle had not rubbed off in the same way that the other sketches on the page had.

Unfortunately, there is no way to prove the age of the brown crayon marks of the bicycle because the page was laminated to keep it safe. Until there is a way to test the sketch, the origins of the bicycle will continue to be a tantalizing mystery.

Like many other Renaissance thinkers, da Vinci set out on a quest for knowledge that carried him throughout his life. Everything fired his imagination. Nothing was too small or too insignificant to capture his attention. The ideas of science and technology that began in the Renaissance continued to move forward, laying the foundation for the great discoveries that were yet to come.

Chapter 7

Danger
and Intrigue

*Mechanical science is most noble and useful above all others, for
by means of it all animated bodies in motion
perform their operations.*

—Leonardo da Vinci[1]

In 1482, Leonardo da Vinci, then thirty years old and a successful artist, longed to see more of the world.[2] He traveled to Milan, hoping to find more work as both an artist and a designer.

Before he left, he sent a letter of introduction to the ruler of Milan, Lodovico Sforza. This remarkable letter, detailing da Vinci's qualifications as a military engineer and artist, gives a glimpse into not only how da Vinci viewed his talents but also the kinds of skills that Renaissance rulers needed in their quests for power.

In the letter, da Vinci first described the kinds of military machines he could build for Sforza, including

Da Vinci wrote that he was talented in many areas, including designing architectural structures, as seen in these sketches of his.

bridges that would be immune to fire attack, siege machines, and vessels for a sea attack. He explained that he knew how to destroy fortresses made of stone and could build underground tunnels for secret attacks. He detailed the kinds of weapons he could build, including mortars that could hurl stones at an enemy. He boasted that he could invent any kind of machine that needed to be made.

In peacetime, da Vinci explained that he could design buildings, develop ways to transport water, and, finally, create artworks, saying, "I can carry out sculpture in marble, bronze, or clay; and also I can do in painting whatever can be done well as any other, be he who he may."[3]

Da Vinci as a Military Engineer

Da Vinci's talent as a skilled military engineer was almost as glorious as his art. His quick mind, his knowledge of scientific concepts, and his boundless imagination made him one of the most respected engineers of the Renaissance. He designed a contraption that looks amazingly like a modern tank. He envisioned dozens of missile machines that could hurl everything from stones to arrows at the enemy. He was obsessed with "multiple effects in his weaponry, [which] led him to [develop] ingenious designs that were the forerunners of modern rapid-firing arms like the machine gun."[4]

Da Vinci's quick mind also came up with ideas that were so far ahead of his time that it would be centuries

In this sketch, da Vinci shows that he has a good deal of military knowledge and imagination.

before anyone understood them. For example, he designed the first helicopter and a very early version of the airplane, neither of which he was ever able to build. It would take another four hundred years before the technology and lightweight materials needed for flight would be invented.

Warfare During the Renaissance

Da Vinci knew that his skills were eagerly sought after by men who longed for power. The men who held power in each Renaissance city-state were not always elected to the position. They often came to power through family ties, political maneuvering, or warfare. Out of the chaos of this struggle for power, one strong man usually emerged who had the power to defeat his opponents and make himself ruler.[5]

The rulers of the city-states were often waging small wars against one another, mostly for land, power, and taxes. So much warfare exhausted the people, so leaders began to hire mercenaries (independent soldiers hired by a ruler to fight a war) to fight their battles for them.[6] Many wars between city-states were no more than skirmishes between hired mercenary groups who were fighting for whoever was paying them.

The Condottieri

These mercenaries were called condottieri. The great majority of condottieri were men of noble birth who had chosen military service as a career.[7] Others were poor men who saw the military as an opportunity to gain fame and fortune.

Some condottieri were so highly regarded that some rulers did not want to lose their services, even in

Da Vinci drew this image of a soldier for hire, or condottiere.

89

peacetime. After Pisa and Florence declared peace after one war, for example, the leaders in Pisa decided not to dismiss the condottieri. The city-state paid them a generous sum and gave them territory won in the war.[8] Other groups of condottieri were little more than bandits. When they were not fighting under contract, these mercenary armies attacked travelers and preyed on ordinary citizens. They demanded protection money, similar to twentieth-century gangsters.[9]

Although the cannon was invented sometime in the early 1300s, most Renaissance battles were fought in much the same way that they had been for hundreds of years. Soldiers, outfitted in heavy armor and carrying massive weapons, fought in hand-to-hand combat on the battlefield. Sometimes, a warrior who wore one of the heavier suits of armor "had to be hoisted by crane onto the back of his horse."[10]

As Italy was invaded by France and other European countries during the last years of the Renaissance, it became clear that the city-states could no longer rely on wandering bands of soldiers for hire. Gradually, organized armies replaced the condottieri, who eventually disappeared.

Military Figures of the Renaissance

During his lifetime, da Vinci would work as an engineer for two of the best-known Renaissance military figures: Lodovico Sforza and Cesare Borgia. These men, although ruthless politicians with a thirst for power, were also true Renaissance men with a love of art and learning. One leader was renowned for his genius and power on the battlefield. The other will always be remembered for one of the Renaissance's worst military blunders.

Lodovico Sforza

Lodovico was the fourth son of Francesco Sforza, a brilliant condottiere who became so powerful that he eventually rose to rule Milan. One Renaissance writer described the Sforza family as "those heroes of patience and cunning who built themselves up from nothing."[11] Francesco's death threw the family into turmoil. For years, family members fought for control of Milan. Finally, in 1481, Lodovico emerged to take his father's place as duke of Milan.

Lodovico Sforza's rule was the golden moment for Milan and the Renaissance. He became a patron of da Vinci for more than twenty years. Sforza funded city projects, built hospitals, and sponsored huge city festivals. Sforza's moment of glory would not last, however.

In the late 1400s, the rulers of Naples planned to attack Milan. At the same time, Sforza heard that the French Army wanted to invade Naples. Because Naples was moving against Sforza and Milan, he supported the French invasion of Naples. He hoped that the French would take the town before its leaders had a chance to move against Milan. So, in an enormous political and military blunder, Sforza let the French troops pass freely through Milanese territory. Soon after, another French army, led by the duke of Orleans, invaded Italy with the intention of taking Milan. Sforza managed to defeat the French, but it was the beginning of the end.

It was not long before the French invaded again. This time, Sforza could not hold them back. The French took Milan and captured Sforza. He died, imprisoned and alone, in 1508.

Cesare Borgia

The illegitimate son of Pope Alexander VI and a Roman courtesan, Borgia was blond, handsome, and so strong that it was said that he could bend a horse-shoe with his bare hands.[12] As a young man he was a member of the clergy, but he left the Catholic Church and began a brilliant military career. First, he allied himself with the French. He was one of the notables who escorted Louis XII into Naples in 1499.[13] Then he began his campaign of conquest through Italy, taking city after city with the desire to reunite them under the Catholic Church. By the time he was twenty-eight, Borgia was one of the most powerful men in the world.

For years, he continued to be involved in wars, fighting his political foes for control. He was suppos-edly as cruel as he was powerful. It is believed that he murdered and poisoned his rivals and anyone he could not defeat in battle. Eventually, however, he was cap-tured by Spanish troops and imprisoned in Spain for two years. He escaped, but not long after, he was killed in battle at age thirty-one.

As shown by the lives of Sforza and Borgia, the Renaissance was a time of bloodshed and war. Then, as today, military leaders longed for the weapons that would give them victory in battle. Although da Vinci was a respected military advisor and the inventor of dozens of deadly military weapons, it is unclear whether any of his inventions was ever built or actually used in battle. What remain are tantalizing hints and detailed drawings of the weapons that his brilliant mind imagined.

Chapter 8

The Renaissance Blooms

The ambitious, who are not content with the gifts of life and the beauty of the world are given the penitence of ruining their own lives and never possessing the utility and beauty of the world.

—Leonardo da Vinci [1]

By the turn of the sixteenth century, da Vinci had reached the pinnacle of his fame. Many of his most famous works had been completed. After years of traveling throughout Italy, from Florence to Rome, he had settled in Milan.

A few years before, in 1499, France had invaded Italy. By the time that da Vinci was in Milan, the city was controlled by the French. They were delighted with da Vinci. To them, he symbolized the values of the Renaissance. In a letter written in 1506, the French governor of Milan, Charles d'Amboise, said of da Vinci, "The excellent works accomplished in Italy and especially in Milan by Master Leonardo da Vinci, your

94

fellow citizen, have made all those who see them singularly love their author, even if they have never met him."[2]

Da Vinci remained in Milan for a number of years, focusing more on engineering and nature than on his painting. He renewed his fascination with anatomy and continued to dissect cadavers. In 1513, with Italy in upheaval from the French invasions and political changes in the Catholic Church, da Vinci moved once again. He hoped to find a powerful patron and protector from the chaos of Italian politics. Eventually, he attached himself to the powerful Medici family. When Giuliano de' Medici died in 1516, the elderly da Vinci found that he was out of style with the new generation of wealthy Italians, who preferred the works of Raphael and Titian. Toward the end of his life, he was without a patron once again.

During this time, Francis I had taken the French throne. Like the rest of France, he was enthralled with da Vinci. He offered patronage to the great Italian Renaissance master, and da Vinci accepted. By the summer of 1517, da Vinci was living in France near the royal château of Amboise.

By this time, the elderly da Vinci could no longer paint, but his mind was still sharp and his brilliance still greatly in demand. The young French king enjoyed da Vinci's company and spent many hours conversing with the old man.

As da Vinci's reputation traveled to the rest of Europe, the ideas of the Renaissance traveled far beyond the Italian borders. Slowly, as the years passed, other countries became enlightened by their own Renaissance movements. As the concepts of humanism, splendor, personal responsibility, and the glorification of the individual took hold, great changes swept through Europe. Nowhere were the concepts of the Renaissance more visible than in three European countries: Germany, France, and England.

The German Renaissance

Germany before the Renaissance was little more than a large collection of separate lands ruled by various dukes, kings, members of the clergy, and powerful individual landowners. Theoretically, the whole country was ruled by one emperor, but the local lords held a great deal of power to wage wars and to run their lands as they chose.

Gradually, the ideas of the Renaissance moved across the Alps into Germany. The German people embraced the ideals of humanism, which became a powerful force in German culture by the early 1500s. Humanist scholars began to see the individual states as a single unified force: Germany.

In Germany, the response to the revival of antiquity that was a hallmark of the Italian Renaissance was scholastic rather than visual.[3] Universities became important centers where the brightest minds debated and influenced the course of the German Renaissance. With the invention of the printing press in Germany in the late 1400s, books by the thousands made their way into even the smallest German villages.

Ideas about religion were affected by the humanist ideas that had been born in Italy years before. One theologian, Martin Luther, embraced the new attitudes about humankind and learning to become one of the most influential thinkers of the age. Like many Renaissance scholars of the day, Luther began studying on his own rather than relying on others for the truth. His studies of the Bible led him to believe that Christ was the mediator between God and humans and that forgiveness of sin came from faith in God, not good works.

This was in direct conflict with the teachings of the Catholic Church, which taught that people controlled their own salvation. Luther's beliefs revolutionized Christianity. Luther is now credited as the father of modern Protestantism, one of the most powerful Christian belief systems in the world.

One of Germany's greatest artists of the Renaissance was Albrecht Dürer. Dürer was born in Nuremberg in 1471, the son of a goldsmith. He was trained in his father's workshop, and in

Martin Luther challenged the power of the Roman Catholic Church and started the Protestant Reformation.

Source Document

It was in the year 1517, when the profligate monk Tetzel, a worthy servant of the pope and the devil—for I am certain that the pope is the agent of the devil on earth—came among us selling indulgences, maintaining their efficacy, and impudently practising on the credulity of the people. When I beheld this unholy and detestable traffic taking place in open day, and thereby sanctioning the most villainous crimes, I could not, though I was then but a young doctor of divinity, refrain from protesting against it in the strongest manner, not only as directly contrary to the Scriptures, but as opposed to the canons of the church itself.[4]

Martin Luther gave this account of his starting the Protestant Reformation in 1517.

1494, when he was only twenty-two, he traveled to Venice. The young German artist was overwhelmed by the city and the vibrancy of the Renaissance. He spent his time studying the great Italian paintings, including those of da Vinci. He was also, like da Vinci, fascinated with nature, botany, and anatomy, and he became one of the first true "universal men" of Germany.

But Dürer's greatest skills lay in woodcuts and engraving. In the art of woodcutting, the artist carves

Albrecht Dürer, whose painting Praying Hands *is seen here, was heavily influenced by the work of the masters of the Renaissance, including Leonardo da Vinci.*

an image into a block of wood, then prints the image on paper. With the invention of the printing press and the explosion of books, Dürer's talents had found a home. There had been professional engravers before him, but he was the first to take the art to its highest achievements. His rich, detailed engravings almost jump off the page. Although he was also a successful painter, it is as a wood engraver that he is the undisputed master.

Francis I and the French Renaissance

With the ascension of Francis I to the French throne in 1515, the splendor of the Renaissance also came to France. Only twenty-one when he became king, Francis I immediately showed his mettle when he invaded and conquered Milan just seven months after he became king. Throughout his life he remained a great admirer of da Vinci and of the ideals of the Renaissance.

His reign, from 1515 to 1547, was marked by intense political struggle and warfare. But his years on the French throne are remembered as the greatest moment of French culture, art, and architecture. Young, handsome, and powerful, Francis I brought so much art into France that one historian remarked, he "had a noble passion for everything beautiful."[5]

The rise of the Renaissance in France mirrored the life and tastes of the young king. While Italy was noted for its philosophy and reverence for history, and Germany was concerned with scholarly pursuits, France loved the vibrant display of wealth, art, and architecture. Francis I spent lavishly and built some of the greatest structures of France. As a true universal man, Francis I also had great respect for the sciences. Not only was he da Vinci's final patron, giving the old master comfort in his final years, but he also founded the College of France.

Eventually, the pressures of war, politics, and finances tarnished the court of Francis I. He struggled to hold his court together under increasing internal strife, but he failed. His finances were in such bad shape that he was forced to sell powerful government jobs to whoever could afford them, which infuriated his political enemies. By the time he died in 1547, the brilliance of his reign was overshadowed by his failures. But his influence on the Renaissance in France is unchallenged.

The Renaissance in England: Elizabeth I and William Shakespeare

The Renaissance came late to England, the British island off the European coast. England had remained a land of small villages for centuries. London, the one large city in England, was far behind the advances of Europe.

The first monarch to embrace the Renaissance was Henry VIII. His notorious reign, from 1509 to 1547, included six wives (two of whom he had beheaded), the founding of the Church of England, and ongoing political unrest within his court and with other countries. Nonetheless, it laid the foundation for a new era of scholarship and art that England had never seen. What Henry began in the first part of the century was fully developed by his daughter, Elizabeth. Of all the great European monarchs of the Renaissance, none is better known than Elizabeth I of England.

Elizabeth ascended the throne in 1558 after the death of her half sister, Mary Tudor. The new queen was faced with a fractured England: divided

Queen Elizabeth I was the most influential figure in the spread of culture and ideas through England.

101

by politics and religion, at war with France, and in danger of conquest. Within a few years, she had firmly established her power as monarch. The young, headstrong woman deftly dispatched political enemies and began lifting her country up to heights of artistic, scholarly, and political power.

Elizabeth's many accomplishments and her overwhelming popularity were a gateway through which the Renaissance entered England. Long after the Renaissance had peaked in Europe, England still enjoyed the effects of a new feeling of individualism and learning as a result of Elizabeth's unshakable faith in her countrymen and her strength as a world leader.

The greatest effect of the Renaissance on England was in the form of communication. The new learning, imported to England through the works of the Italian humanists and their respect for the classics, transformed the country. English, once a language considered ugly and common, began being used more and more as the language of English scholars and thinkers. New words from Latin, Greek, Italian, and French crept into the English language. The Renaissance added between ten thousand and twelve thousand new words to English.[6]

It was in the field of drama that the English Renaissance found its clearest and deepest expression.[7] Drama's greatest individual was William Shakespeare. This Elizabethan playwright is undeniably the most important figure in the English

Source Document

To be, or not to be: that is the question:
Whether 'tis nobler in the mind to suffer
The slings and arrows of outrageous fortune,
Or to take arms against a sea of troubles,
And by opposing end them? To die: to sleep;
No more; and by a sleep to say we end
The heart-ache and the thousand natural shocks
That flesh is heir to, 'tis a consummation
Devoutly to be wish'd. To die, to sleep;
To sleep: perchance to dream: ay, there's the rub;
For in that sleep of death what dreams may come
When we have shuffled off this mortal coil,
Must give us pause: there's the respect
That makes calamity of so long life;
For who would bear the whips and scorns of time,
The oppressor's wrong, the proud man's
    contumely,
The pangs of despised love, the law's delay,
The insolence of office and the spurns
That patient merit of the unworthy takes,
When he himself might his quietus make
With a bare bodkin?. . .[8]

William Shakespeare remains the best-known figure of the English Renaissance, and probably the most famous writer in the history of the English language. This is an excerpt from his tragic play Hamlet.

Renaissance and perhaps in the history of the English language.

There is very little hard documentation of Shakespeare's life. Eighteenth-century scholar George Stevens wrote,

> All that is known with any degree of certainty concerning Shakespeare is that he was born in Stratford-upon-Avon, married and had children there, went to London where he . . . wrote poems and plays, returned to Stratford, made his will, died, and was buried.[9]

This statement is quite true. More than two hundred years after Stevens made that comment, only a few legal documents, some first-person accounts, and, most importantly, Shakespeare's plays are all that is left to the world.

Many of the plays that exist have come down through history in what is known as the First Folio, a collection of his plays, which is the earliest known printing of Shakespeare's work. However, he wrote his plays to be performed, not read. He apparently had no hand in their publication.[10]

Shakespeare's brilliance as a playwright and author lies in the fact that he made the English language a thing of beauty. He embraced the new Renaissance way of thinking about the world and turned it into a celebration of language. He introduced to the world such words as *accommodation, assassination, obscene,* and *submerged.* Phrases that are used every day, such as "It is Greek to me,"

"Something is rotten in the state of Denmark," and "method to the madness," have their origins in Shakespeare's works.[11]

Both Shakespeare and Elizabeth died in the early years of the seventeenth century, but their influence was felt for generations afterward. Today, plays, movies, and books continue to be written about both of them, testifying to the power of their personalities and to the impact they had on the Renaissance world—and the world today.

Like them, da Vinci's life had a tremendous impact on the world. His brilliance influenced politicians, kings, and Popes both during his lifetime and long after his death.

Chapter 9

The Light Fades

Just as a well-filled day brings blessed sleep,
so a well-employed life brings a blessed death.

—Leonardo da Vinci [1]

By the spring of 1519, da Vinci was sixty-seven years old. He was comfortably settled in Amboise. He had spent the last few years in the company of Francis I, continuing his studies of nature and science, and occasionally busying himself with court festivities.

In April, he wrote his will. In it, he made arrangements for his funeral, stating that he desired "to be buried within the church of Saint Florentin in Amboise and that . . . Sixty tapers shall be carried which shall be borne by sixty poor men, to whom shall be given money for carrying them."[2] He goes on to bequeath his gardens to his servants, a cloak to his waiting woman, and all the rest—his notebooks,

106

Leonardo da Vinci drew this self-portrait in his later years.

clothing, writing, and instruments—to Francesco Melzi of Milan, da Vinci's friend and heir.

Less than a month later, on May 2, 1519, the great Leonardo da Vinci died. A story, first told by the biographer Giorgio Vasari, describes how the French king had entered da Vinci's bedchamber just as the priest had finished last rites, a Catholic ritual in which a dying person can make a final confession of sins. Da Vinci, weak and dying, raised himself on his bed and lamented how he had "offended God by not working on his art as much as he should have."[3] The king took the dying da Vinci in his arms and held him until the last breath left his body.

This romantic idea of da Vinci's death persisted for decades, until a French scholar named Leon de Laborde tried to prove that the king was really elsewhere on the day that da Vinci died. Scholars continue to debate the story, but most agree that the king most likely was not present during da Vinci's last minutes.

The Waning of the Renaissance

The decline of the Renaissance in Europe, like da Vinci's last years, was gradual. And like da Vinci's later life in France, the Italy of the Renaissance would be influenced by foreigners.

The French invasion of Italy did not signal the end of the Renaissance, but it was the first piercing look into the future. The northern Italian provinces had been so devastated by war that English envoys advised Henry VIII to leave them alone. Genoa had been pillaged, Milan had been taxed too heavily, Rome had been sacked, and Florence had been starved and financially ruined.[4] The only city to escape the ravages was Venice.

Italy was ripe for invasion, and other countries began carving up the once-great city-states. Milan became a Spanish area, ruled by a Spanish viceroy. Other Italian cities such as Florence, Naples, Sicily, and Mantua also came under Spanish protection.

But it was not simply foreign control that sent Italy into decline. It was some of the very technology that the Renaissance encouraged that helped seal Italy's fate. In 1488, the first ships rounded the Cape of Good Hope, opening a sea route to India.[5] Transporting goods over this route was much cheaper than overland travel to Venice. Gradually, the grand trade city declined. Also, the discovery of the New World turned Europe's attention from Italy to the newly powerful Spain and Portugal. Their Atlantic shores became shipping centers. The vast riches of the Americas began pouring into them.

The final nail in the coffin of the Renaissance was the continued decline of the Roman Catholic Church. With the rise of Martin Luther's beliefs and the religion of Protestantism, the church's power began to slip away. In desperation, the church began to tighten its grip on everything it could. It also began censoring books that did not fit in with its teachings. The Renaissance freedom of expression and search for new ideas was gradually buried under the weight of censorship and fear.

This is not to say that all learning stopped as the Renaissance declined. Great advances in science, art, and technology were just around the corner. But the glory days of the Italian Renaissance, when the universal man was revered, were over.

The Renaissance's Effect on Society

The idea that the individual was capable of shaping his or her own destiny, the basic tenet of humanism, became the basis for almost everything that was to come afterward. As a result, the excitement of the Renaissance could not be completely extinguished, and progress continued to be made in all parts of society.

In medicine and science, scholars continued to experiment and learn about the natural world. Astronomers built upon the work of Copernicus and continued to watch the sky. Physicians, many of whom had studied in the great Italian universities, were freer to experiment and study the human body by dissection. The trade routes moved from Venice to Spain, and merchants who invested in trade with the New World grew rich.

In religion, there was a growing population of Protestants throughout Europe who wanted to practice their faith as they saw fit. Persecuted by the Catholic Church, other branches of Protestantism, and society, these people—believing in the rights of the individual that were so important to the Renaissance—fled to the New World to find religious freedom.

Cities such as Florence continued their traditions of artistic patronage. City leaders and the church continued to support artists, but there was neither the desire nor the funds to support the great works that had been achieved during the Renaissance.

The Fate of da Vinci's Notebooks

When da Vinci died, his friend and heir, Francesco Melzi, became the owner of all of da Vinci's written manuscripts. The biographer Vasari claims to have seen them, saying that Melzi "guarded them as though they were relics."[6] Melzi went through the writings and extracted passages that da Vinci had written on the subject of painting. He eventually published the random instructions in a book called *Treatise on Painting*.

When Metzi died in 1570, he left his priceless collection to his son Orazio. Orazio did not have the same reverence for the late master's works. He began selling them as fast as he could. Notebooks and unbound sheets were soon scattered all over the world. No one kept complete records of where they all went. Many known works were lost. Others have been handed down for generations with care and reverence. Today, da Vinci's notebooks can be seen in the collections of such great museums as the Metropolitan Museum in New York, the Louvre in Paris, the

Victoria and Albert Museum in London, and the Uffizi in Florence.

Historians believe that less than two thirds of da Vinci's manuscripts have survived.[7] More than five thousand pages from the original thirteen thousand are lost. Occasionally, however, scholars are surprised by a new find. In 1965, for example, two presumed lost manuscripts were discovered tucked away on a forgotten shelf in the National Library of Madrid. These works include most of da Vinci's work on the bronze horse and on military machines, and they are a priceless resource on this part of his work.

In November 1994, one of da Vinci's manuscripts, the Codex Leicester, was auctioned. This notebook, filled with his notes about astronomy, the sun, and the sky, was quickly snapped up by an anonymous bidder for a record $30 million. The sale stunned the art world. Not only was it the most money ever paid for a work of art other than a painting, but it was also the most ever paid for a manuscript and the tenth most expensive object ever sold at auction.

For days, no one knew who had bought the precious document. Then it was announced: Bill Gates, the cofounder of Microsoft, was the new owner of da Vinci's priceless work. He immediately sent the document on a world tour and created an elaborate CD-ROM of the notebook. Many art scholars cringed at the idea that Gates would make money off the rare work. However, Gates has apparently held his new

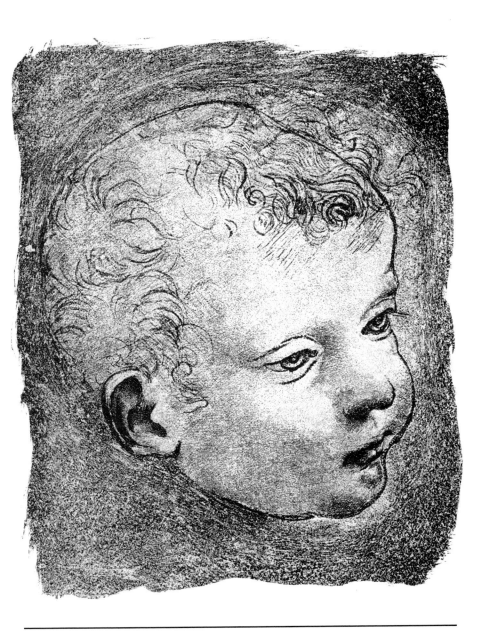

Da Vinci's artistic and scientific talents are clear on every page of his notebooks.

possession in as high regard as those who have owned it before him.

Restoration of *The Last Supper*

Another of da Vinci's works that has been snatched from destruction is his masterpiece *The Last Supper*. The fresco (a large work painted on wet plaster) depicts the Passover meal the night before Christ was crucified. The painting is a brilliant study of human emotion. Unfortunately, da Vinci was experimenting with a new painting technique as he painted *The Last Supper*. The work had begun to deteriorate even before he was finished. Fifty years later, it was described as "a dazzling stain."[8]

Remarkably, the fresco has survived. At one point, a doorway was cut through the bottom of the fresco, destroying the area beneath Christ's feet. During World War II, the building housing the painting was nearly completely destroyed by bombs—except for the one wall on which the fresco was painted, which the monks had carefully protected.

In 1977, the most ambitious restoration project ever attempted got under way. For twenty-two years, restorers painstakingly cleaned the fresco, which had been blackened by decades of dirt and grime. Finally, in May 1999, a brighter, cleaner *Last Supper* was unveiled.

The restoration revealed new life and color, but critics blasted the work from the moment it was revealed. James Beck, an art history professor at

Da Vinci's The Last Supper *is one of the most famous paintings in the world. Despite the amazing task of restoration, it is still difficult to reproduce clearly.*

Columbia University, was quoted as saying, "It is 20 percent Leonardo and 80 percent restoration."[9] Some art historians were appalled at the idea that the restoration might have removed earlier paint, some of which might have been closer to mimicking original— and now lost—parts of the work.

Regardless of some critics' dismay at the restoration, the fact remains that the new *Last Supper* glows with a light that has not been seen in generations. Fruit on the table, which had previously been hidden under grime, now seem juicy enough to eat. Small details, such as facial expressions and the colors of the robes, shine. Although it might not be completely da Vinci's, *The Last Supper* is still a powerful masterwork from a Renaissance genius.

Chapter 10

Legacy

Although the glory of the Renaissance has faded, its ideals have never been extinguished. The idea that people had the right to control their own lives became accepted as a normal fact of life. Like the people of the Renaissance, the Founding Fathers of the United States looked to the democratic ideals of ancient Greece and Rome, among others, as they put together the government of the fledgling United States in the late 1700s. The idea that people had a right to live as they wished, to worship as they wished, and to have the right to "life, liberty, and the pursuit of happiness" comes, in part, from the ideals Italy embraced during the age of the Renaissance.

Like the ideals of the time in which he lived, Leonardo da Vinci's impact on the world is incalculable. His revolutionary ideas about science,

Like the great thinkers of the Renaissance, the American founders, including George Washington, Thomas Jefferson, James Madison, and John Adams, looked to the democratic ideals of ancient Greece and Rome for inspiration.

technology, and natural history kept the light of knowledge burning long after the Renaissance faded. Likewise, his art still has the power to inspire all who see it.

In one of his notebooks, da Vinci described walking into a cave in the countryside. He wrote, "I leaned to one side, then the other, to see if I could distinguish anything, but the great darkness within made this impossible. After a time there rose in me both fear and desire—fear of the dark and menacing cave; desire to see whether it contained some marvelous thing."[1] The Renaissance was a time when, like da Vinci, the world peered into the dark cave of the past and indeed saw marvelous things. As long as the world remains unafraid to explore and discover, the legacy of Leonardo da Vinci and the other daring people of the Renaissance will always live on.

Timeline

1452—Leonardo da Vinci is born on April 15 to Ser Piero da Vinci, a notary, and Caterina.

1453—Constantinople is invaded by the Turks; Greek scholars flee to Italy.

1469—Lorenzo de' Medici becomes ruler of Florence.

1471—First European observatory is founded in Nuremberg.

1472—Da Vinci joins the painter's guild in Florence; Dante's *Commedia* (The Divine Comedy) is published.

1473–1475—Da Vinci contributes an angel to a painting by Andrea del Verrocchio.

1474—The first book printed in English is published, *The Game and Play of the Chess.*

1475—Michelangelo is born.

1480—Lodovico Sforza takes power in Milan; Birth of Martin Luther.

1481—Da Vinci paints *Adoration of the Magi.*

1484—Sandro Botticelli paints *The Birth of Venus.*

1491—Henry VIII of England is born.

1492—Lorenzo de' Medici dies; Columbus lands in the New World.

1493—Da Vinci's clay model horse goes on display in Milan.

1494—The Italian Wars begin with France invading Italy; Albrecht Dürer visits Venice.

1498—Da Vinci finishes *The Last Supper*; Explorer Vasco da Gama discovers a sea route to India.

1499—The French again invade Italy and take Milan.

1499—Cesare Borgia conquers parts of Italy.
–1503

1501—The French occupy Rome.

1503—Da Vinci paints the *Mona Lisa*.
–1505

1504—Michelangelo completes his statue of *David*; Da Vinci's father dies.

1508—Michelangelo paints the ceiling of the Sistine Chapel.
–1512

1513—Niccolò Machiavelli writes *The Prince*, but it is not published until 1532.

1515—Francis I of France invades Italy.

1517—Da Vinci arrives in France; Martin Luther publishes his Ninety-five Theses, setting off the Protestant Reformation, which will challenge the power of the Roman Catholic Church.

1519—Da Vinci dies on May 2.

1542—The Inquisition begins in Rome.

1543—Nicolaus Copernicus publishes his ideas about the solar system; Andreas Vesalius publishes a book on anatomy.

1564—Michelangelo dies.

Chapter Notes

Chapter 1. Buried Treasure in Their Own House

1. Paul Robert Walker, *The Italian Renaissance* (New York: Facts on File, 1995), p. viii.
2. John R. Hale, *Renaissance* (New York: Time-Life Books, 1965), p. 16.

Chapter 2. Life in a New World

1. Ladislao Reti, ed., *Unknown Leonardo* (New York: McGraw-Hill, 1974), p. 10.
2. Ibid., p. 9.
3. Will Durant, *The Renaissance: A History of Civilization in Italy from 1304–1576* (New York: Simon and Schuster, 1953), p. 199.
4. Paul Halsall, "Medieval Sourcebook: Petrus Paulus Vergerius: The New Education (c. 1400)," *Internet Medieval Sourcebook*, March 1996, <http://www.fordham.edu/halsall/source/vergerius.html> (October 30, 1999).
5. Stephen Pumfrey, ed., *Science, Culture, and Popular Belief in Renaissance Europe* (England: Manchester University Press, 1991), pp. 22–23.
6. John Gage, *Life in Italy at the Time of the Medici* (New York: G. P. Putnam's Sons, 1968), p. 25.
7. Durant, p. 578.
8. Ibid., p. 587.
9. Charles Panati, *Extraordinary Origins of Everyday Things* (New York: Harper & Row, 1987), p. 22.
10. Gage, p. 26.
11. Ibid., p. 106.
12. E. R. Chamberlin, *Everyday Life in Renaissance Times* (New York: G. P. Putnam's Sons, 1965), p. 102.
13. Jacob Bruckhardt, *The Civilization of the Renaissance in Italy* (New York: Harper & Row, 1958), vol. 2, pp. 382–383.
14. Ibid., p. 224.
15. Ibid.

Chapter 3. City Life

1. Ladislao Reti, ed., *Unknown Leonardo* (New York: McGraw-Hill, 1974), p. 298.

2. Giorgio Vasari, *Lives of the Artists*, ed. Betty Burroughs (New York: Simon and Schuster, 1946), pp. 187–188.

3. Will Durant, *The Renaissance: A History of Civilization in Italy from 1304–1576* (New York: Simon and Schuster, 1953), p. 133.

4. John Gage, *Life in Italy at the Time of the Medici* (New York: G. P. Putnam's Sons, 1968), p. 70.

5. Robert Wallace, *The World of Leonardo, 1452–1519* (New York: Time-Life Books, 1966), p. 14.

6. E. R. Chamberlin, *Everyday Life in Renaissance Times* (New York: G. P. Putnam's Sons, 1965), p. 87.

7. Gage, p. 120.

8. Ibid., p. 104.

9. Chamberlin, p. 73.

10. Durant, p. 530.

11. Paul Robert Walker, *The Italian Renaissance* (New York: Facts on File, 1995), p. 48.

12. Ibid., p. 21.

13. Jacob Bruckhardt, *The Civilization of the Renaissance in Italy* (New York: Harper & Row, 1958), vol. 11, p. 186.

Chapter 4. Beauty in a Beautiful World

1. Ladislao Reti, ed., *Unknown Leonardo* (New York: McGraw-Hill, 1974), p. 293.

2. Jean Paul Richter, ed., *The Notebook of Leonardo da Vinci* (New York: Dover Publications, Inc., 1970), vol. 2, p. 326.

3. Giorgio Vasari, *Lives of the Artists*, ed. Betty Burroughs (New York: Simon and Schuster, 1946), p. 195.

4. Ludwig Goldscheider, *Leonardo Da Vinci* (London: Phaidon Press, 1959), p. 37.

5. Vasari, pp. 195–196.

6. Bruno Santi, *Leonardo Da Vinci* (New York: Scala Books, 1990), p. 34.

7. Vasari, p. 194.

8. Roy McMullen, *Mona Lisa: The Picture and the Myth* (New York: Da Capo Press, 1977), p. 209.

9. Ibid., p. 158.

10. Reti, pp. 88–90.

11. Ibid., p. 92.

12. Vasari, p. 149.

13. Ibid., p. 297.

14. Ibid., p. 269.

15. Frederick Hartt, *History of Renaissance Art* (New York: Harry Abrams, 1994), p. 468.

16. Ibid., pp. 508–509.

Chapter 5. Knowledge Is Power

1. Ladislao Reti, ed., *Unknown Leonardo* (New York: McGraw-Hill, 1974), p. 293.

2. Serge Bramly, *Leonardo: The Artist and the Man* (New York: Penguin Books, 1994), p. 83.

3. Eugenio Garin, *Italian Humanism: Philosophy and Civic Life in the Renaissance* (New York: Harper and Row, 1965), P. 7.

4. Will Durant, *The Renaissance: A History of Civilization in Italy from 1304–1576* (New York: Simon and Schuster, 1953), p. 77.

5. Jacob Bruckhardt, *The Civilization of the Renaissance in Italy* (New York: Harper and Row, 1958), vol. 2, p. 148.

6. Paul Robert Walker, *The Italian Renaissance* (New York: Facts on File, 1995), pp. 37–38.

7. Ibid., pp. 10–11.

8. Durant, pp. 210–211.

9. Paul Halsall, "Medieval Sourcebook: Nicolo Machiavelli (1469–1527): The Prince, 1513," *Medieval Source Book*, July 1998, <http://www.fordham.edu/halsall/basis/machiavelli-prince.html> (September 30, 1999).

10. Durant, p. 556.

11. E. R. Chamberlin, *Everyday Life in Renaissance Times* (New York: G. P. Putnam's Sons, 1965), p. 161.

12. Ibid., p. 163.

Chapter 6. A World of New Ideas

1. Ladislao Reti, ed., *Unknown Leonardo* (New York: McGraw-Hill, 1974), p. 299.

2. Serge Bramly, *Leonardo: The Artist and the Man* (New York: Penguin Books, 1988), p. 258.

3. Museum of Science, "Leonardo Da Vinci: Scientist, Inventor, Artist," art exhibit, Boston, 1997.

4. Stephen Pumfrey, ed., *Science, Culture, and Popular Belief in Renaissance Europe* (England: University of Manchester Press, 1991), pp. 48–49.

5. E. R. Chamberlin, *Everyday Life in Renaissance Times* (New York: G. P. Putnam's Sons, 1965), p. 20.

6. Pumfrey, pp. 177–178.

7. Chamberlin, p. 23.

8. Ibid., pp. 170–171.

9. Pumfrey, p. 191.

10. Will Durant, *The Renaissance: A History of Civilization in Italy from 1304–1576* (New York: Simon and Schuster, 1953), p. 532.

11. Chamberlin, p. 172.

12. Ibid., p. 168.

13. Jacob Bruckhardt, *The Civilization of the Renaissance in Italy* (New York: Harper and Row, 1958), vol. 2, p. 287.

Chapter 7. Danger and Intrigue

1. Ladislao Reti, ed., *Unknown Leonardo* (New York: McGraw-Hill, 1974), p. 296.

2. Will Durant, *The Renaissance: A History of Civilization in Italy from 1304–1576* (New York: Simon and Schuster, 1953), p. 202.

3. Ludwig Goldscheider, *Leonardo Da Vinci* (London: Phaidon Press, 1969), p. 33.

4. Reti, p. 184.

5. Durant, p. 174.

6. H. W. Koch, *Medieval Warfare* (New York: Prentice-Hall, 1978), p. 174.

7. Eugenio Garin, *Italian Humanism: Philosophy and Civic Life in the Renaissance* (New York: Harper and Row, 1965), p. 30.

8. Koch, p. 175.

9. Paul Robert Walker, *The Italian Renaissance* (New York: Facts on File, 1995), p. 13.

10. E. R. Chamberlin, *Everyday Life in Renaissance Times* (New York, G. P. Putnam's Sons, 1965), p. 154.

11. Koch, p. 198.

12. Durant, p. 417.

13. Ibid., p. 419.

Chapter 8. The Renaissance Blooms

1. Ladislao Reti, ed., *Unknown Leonardo* (New York: McGraw-Hill, 1974), p. 300.

2. Quoted in Serge Bramly, *Leonardo: The Artist and the Man* (New York: Penguin Books, 1988), p. 355.

3. Erwin Panofsky, *The Life and Art of Albrecht Dürer* (Princeton, N.J.: Princeton University Press, 1955), p. 30.

4. Martin Luther, "Martin Luther Protests Against the Sale of Indulgences, Wittenberg, Germany, 1517," *The Mammoth Book of Eyewitness History*, ed. Jon E. Lewis (New York: Carroll & Graf Publishers, Inc., 1998), pp. 103–104.

5. Denys Hay, ed., *The Age of the Renaissance* (New York: McGraw-Hill Book Company, 1967), p. 164.

6. Robert Crum, William Cran, and Robert MacNeil, *The Story of English* (New York: Viking Penguin, 1986), p. 95.

7. Hay, p. 265.

8. William Shakespeare, *Hamlet*, Act III, Scene I.

9. Crum, Cran, and MacNeil, p. 100.

10. *Grolier's Multimedia Encyclopedia* (Bethel, Conn.: Grolier Interactive, 1999).

11. Crum, Cran, and MacNeil, p. 99.

Chapter 9. The Light Fades

1. Serge Bramly, *Leonardo: The Artist and the Man* (New York: Penguin Books, 1988), p. 407.

2. Ladislao Reti, ed., *Unknown Leonardo* (New York: McGraw-Hill, 1974), p. 19.

3. Bramly, p. 407.

4. Will Durant, *The Renaissance: A History of Civilization in Italy from 1304–1576* (New York: Simon and Schuster, 1953), p. 686.

5. Ibid., p. 687.

6. Wallace, p. 169.

7. Bramly, p. 420.

8. Ibid., p. 296.

9. Piero Valsecchi, "A Bright, New Look at Leonardo's 'Last Supper,'" *Seattle Times*, May 27, 1999, <http://seattletimes.com/news/entertainment/html98/supp-19990527.html>.

Chapter 10. Legacy

1. Ladislao Reti, ed., *Unknown Leonardo* (New York: McGraw-Hill, 1974), p. 293.

Further Reading

Books

Bramly, Serge. *Leonardo: The Artist and the Man.* New York: Penguin Books, 1988.

Pinguill, Yves. *Da Vinci: The Painter Who Spoke with Birds.* New York: Chelsea House Publishers, 1994.

Richter, Jean Paul. *The Notebooks of Leonardo da Vinci.* 2 vols. New York: Dover Publications, Inc., 1970.

Santi, Bruno. *The Library of Great Masters: Leonardo Da Vinci.* New York: Riverside Books, 1990.

Walker, Paul Robert. *The Italian Renaissance.* New York: Facts on File, 1995.

Internet Addresses

American Museum of Natural History. *Leonardo's Codex Leicester: A Masterpiece of Science.* 1998. <http://www.amnh.org/exhibitions/codex/index.html> (April 14, 2000).

Leonardo da Vinci Museum. n.d. <http://www.davinci-museum.com/> (April 14, 2000).

"Leonardo da Vinci." *Web Museum, Paris.* May 20, 1996. <http://metalab.unc.edu/wm/paint/auth/vinci/> (April 14, 2000).

Soojung-Kim Pang, Alex. *Humanism and the Scientific Revolution.* 1996. <http://pubweb.ucdavis.edu/documents/ASPANG/Modern/Humanism.html> (April 14, 2000).

Index